THE BRITISH ACADEMY

Modern Research as illustrating the Bible

By

The Rev. S. R. Driver, D.D., Litt.D.

Regius Professor of Hebrew
and Canon of Christ Church, Oxford
Fellow of the British Academy

The Schweich Lectures

1908

Wipf & Stock
PUBLISHERS
Eugene, Oregon

Wipf and Stock Publishers
199 W 8th Ave, Suite 3
Eugene, OR 97401

Modern Research as illustrating the Bible
The Schweich Lectures 1908
By Driver, Samuel R.
ISBN 13: 978-1-55635-452-6
ISBN 10: 1-55635-452-5
Publication date 5/1/2007
Previously published by The British Academy / Oxford University Press, UK, 1909

PREFATORY NOTE

THE Schweich Trust was founded in 1907 in memory of the late Mr. Leopold Schweich, of Paris. The £10,000 constituting the Trust was handed over to the British Academy, which agreed to accept and administer the Trust. The Trust Fund is to be devoted 'to the furtherance of research in the archaeology, art, history, languages, and literature of Ancient Civilization with reference to Biblical Study'; and a portion of the annual income of the Trust has been appropriated to providing not less than three lectures to be delivered annually on some subject coming within the scope of the objects which the Trust is intended to promote. The Council of the British Academy having done me the honour of inviting me to deliver the introductory course of Schweich Lectures, I thought that a suitable line for me to take would be, firstly (Lecture I) to give some account of the progress that had been made during the past century in the principal branches of research enumerated in the Trust deed, and afterwards (Lectures II and III) to give an outline of the new knowledge respecting Palestine which had been obtained recently, partly from inscriptions, and partly from the excavations in Palestine itself, which had formed during the last ten years such an important and interesting development of archaeological investigation. It will be understood that in my accounts of the excavations in Palestine I am dependent entirely upon the reports given by the excavators themselves. I have endeavoured to summarize, as well as I could within the limits at my disposal, the principal results which had been gained: but it must be remembered that, where there are no inscriptions telling us distinctly what the objects found were, mistakes are possible, and some of the conclusions reached may in the light of further knowledge have to be revised. I have ventured here and there to indicate conclusions which ought perhaps for the present to be regarded as provisional. An adequate account of the pottery of Palestine, and of the sometimes difficult questions arising in connexion with it, even had it been within my power to give it, obviously could not be included; perhaps it may be found to form a suitable subject to be dealt with by an expert in some subsequent course of Schweich Lectures.

My second and third Lectures were illustrated by lantern-slides. The illustrations in the present volume will, I hope, enable readers to realize, better than they could otherwise do, the nature of the places and objects described; the majority are selected from those shown at the Lectures, but some are new. In most cases I am indebted to the publishers of the books from which they are taken for granting me facilities for their reproduction; but a few of those taken from foreign publications are based upon negatives taken here for the lantern-slides from the publications themselves. The blocks for three of the illustrations from *Tell Ta'annek* were very kindly lent me by the Philosophical and Historical Department of the Vienna Academy of Sciences; the other illustrations from the same volume were obtained from negatives taken in the first instance for the purpose just mentioned. I must also in conclusion express my indebtedness to Mr. Stanley A. Cook, Lecturer in Hebrew and Syriac at Gonville and Caius College, Cambridge, and editor of the *Quarterly Statement* of the Palestine Exploration Fund, for reading my second and third Lectures in proof, and offering me out of his wide knowledge of the archaeology of Palestine various criticisms and suggestions which I have in most cases gratefully utilized.

S. R. DRIVER.

CHRIST CHURCH, OXFORD.
  December 17, 1908.

CONTENTS

LECTURE I

SKETCH OF THE PROGRESS OF RESEARCH DURING THE PAST CENTURY 1

Part I. Sketch of the principal departments of research bearing on the Bible, pursued during the past century (pp. 1-16).

Rise of the spirit of research, 1; light thrown on Greek and Roman civilization by the discovery of inscriptions and papyri, and by excavation of historical sites, 2; decipherment of Egyptian and Assyrian inscriptions, both begun in 1802, leading to the rediscovery of two great and important civilizations of antiquity, 3-7; Phoenician, Aramaic, and ancient Arabic inscriptions, variously illustrating the Old Testament, 7; travel and exploration in Palestine, 8-9; foundation of the Palestine Exploration Fund and the German Palästina-Verein, 9; scientific surveys of Palestine and Sinai, 9; excavation in Palestine since 1890, 10; rise of the science of textual criticism, and philological study of the languages of the Bible, 11-14; idioms of the New Testament illustrated from inscriptions and papyri, 14; light thrown upon the relation of the Hebrews to their neighbours by the study of inscriptions, 15.

Part II. Illustrations of the gain to Biblical science from the discoveries of the last sixty years (pp. 16-31).

The tribute of Jehu, mentioned on the 'Black Obelisk' of Shalmaneser II, 16-17; Hoshea raised to the throne by Tiglath-Pileser III, 18; Sargon ascertained to be the conqueror of Samaria, 18; detailed particulars of the campaign in which Sennacherib attacked Jerusalem, 19; the chronology of the Books of Kings rectified by the Assyrian annals, 20; the Inscription of Mesha (the 'Moabite Stone'), 21; the Creation and Deluge tablets, discovered in 1872-3 by George Smith, 22, 23; illustrations of Acts xix from inscriptions found in 1877 at Ephesus, 23, 24; prevalent ideas respecting Belshazzar, Cyrus, and Darius the Mede corrected by inscriptions published in 1880 by Mr. Pinches, 25; light thrown recently on the early dynasties of Babylon, 26; sites of Pithom and Goshen determined in 1883 and 1885 by M. Naville, 26; Code of Ḥammurabi, discovered at Susa in 1901, 26-7; documents revealing the existence of a Jewish colony settled at Elephantine in Upper Egypt in the fifth century B.C., discovered in 1904 by Dr. Mond, 28; petition sent by this colony to the Persian governor of Jerusalem in 408 B.C. for permission to rebuild their temple, discovered in 1907, 29; discovery in 1906 and 1907 of Hittite and Babylonian inscriptions at Boghaz-keui in Asia Minor, the old capital of the Hittites, 31.

LECTURE II

CANAAN, AS KNOWN THROUGH INSCRIPTIONS AND EXCAVATION . 32

The Tell el-Amarna tablets, discovered in 1887, 32; light thrown by them upon the political relations of Western Asia, and the condition of

Canaan in the fifteenth century B.C., 33-7; expeditions through Canaan of Thothmes III, 33; of Seti I and Rameses II, 37; treaty of Rameses II with the Hittites, 37-8; mention made of various places in Canaan in *The Travels of a Mohar*, written in the reign of Rameses II, 38; Merenptah, probably the Pharaoh of the Exodus, mentions the capture of places in Canaan, and the 'desolation' of Israel, 38-9.

Excavation in Canaan: principal places excavated, 40, 41; Tell el-Ḥesy, the 'mound of many cities', 41, 42; contains the remains of eleven cities, dating from 1700 B.C. to 400 B.C., resting one upon another, 41-5; in all probability the site of the ancient Lachish, 45, 46; Gezer, discovery of its site by Clermont-Ganneau, 46; its strategic importance, 47; notices of Gezer in the Old Testament, 45-6; seven strata of remains at Gezer, 49; two lowest strata, belonging to the Neolithic age, 49; inhabitants at this time cave-dwellers, character of their civilization, 51-3; third and fourth strata, dating from about 2000 to 1200 B.C., 53; indications of an Egyptian settlement in the south-east of Palestine between 2000 and 1800 B.C., 53-4; the city-walls of Gezer, 54-6; figures of the Phoenician goddess Ashtōreth (Astarte) found at Gezer in the fourth stratum, 56-7; her worship in other parts of Canaan and elsewhere, 57-9.

LECTURE III

CANAAN, AS KNOWN THROUGH INSCRIPTIONS AND EXCAVATION (*continued*) 60

High places, notices of them in the Old Testament, and what they were, 60-1; high place on the rocks above Petra, 61-2; high place of Gezer, with *maẓẓēbāhs* (standing-stones, or 'pillars'), 62-5; standing-stones found elsewhere in Canaan, 65; remains of high places at Mizpah, Gibeon, and other ancient sites in Canaan, 65-7; jars containing bones of infants found at Gezer, Taanach, and Megiddo, 68; fifth and sixth strata represent the period of the Israelite occupation of Canaan, 69; skeletons found buried under walls at Gezer, Taanach, and Megiddo, 69-70; foundation sacrifices, 71, 72; lamp and bowl deposits, their supposed symbolism, 72-3; tombs of unusual type, perhaps those of Philistines, discovered at Gezer, 73-4; stamped jar-handles, found at Tell eṣ-Ṣāfi and other places, possibly the work of the royal potters mentioned in 1 Chron. iv. 23, 74-7; numerous Rhodian wine-jars found at Sandaḥannah, testifying to trade with Rhodes in the third and second centuries B.C., 77 f.; cuneiform tablets, dating from 651 and 648 B.C., found at Gezer, 78; seventh stratum, containing remains of the Maccabaean period, 78; discovery of the castle built by Simon Maccabaeus in 143 B.C., 78-80; Prof. Sellin's excavations at Taanach, 80-6; cuneiform letters addressed to Ishtar-washur, ruler of Taanach, in the fourteenth century B.C., 82-3; elaborately constructed incense-altar found there, 84-5; summary of results of excavation as regards both the history of material civilization in Canaan and religious practices and beliefs, 86-90; importance of continuing it, 90-1; excavation of the walls of Jericho, 91-2.

LIST OF ILLUSTRATIONS

The Rock of Behistun, showing the Trilingual Inscription of Darius . . . . *To face page*	4
The Black Obelisk of Shalmaneser II . . . . ,,	16
The Tribute of Jehu as represented on the Black Obelisk . . ,,	17
Ḥammurabi, King of Babylon, receiving his Laws from the Sun-god ,,	26
Head of Mummy of Rameses II. . . . . . . *Between pages* 38 *and*	39
Granite Bust of Merenptah . . . . . . ,, ,,	39
Map of South-west Judah, showing the Sites excavated	40
The Mound of Tell el-Ḥesy, from the North-east, showing the part excavated . . . . *To face page*	41
Rooms in a Castle at Megiddo . . . . ,,	42
Section of the part of Tell el-Ḥesy excavated by Dr. Bliss . . .	43
Sennacherib receiving the Spoil of Lachish . . . . *To face page*	45
Boundary-inscriptions of Gezer	46
View of Tell ej-Jezer from the South . . . . . *To face page*	47
Plan of Gezer, as exposed by excavation	48
Plan of the Neolithic Burial-cave	50
Jar from the Burial-cave, containing an Infant's Bones . . *To face page*	50
Cup-marks in Rock-surface above three large Caves . . . ,,	51
The Rubbing-stone	52
The Excavation of Gezer in Progress . . . . *Between pages* 54 *and*	55
Clay Figure of Astarte from Taanach . . . . . *To face page*	57
Terra-cotta Figure of Astarte from Cyprus . . . . ,,	57
Astarte Figure, of peculiar type, from Taanach . . . . ,,	57
Astarte-Plaque, of Egyptian type, from Gezer	57
Possible Horned Astarte from Gezer . . . . . *To face page*	58
Clay Figure of Astarte found at Taanach . . . . . ,,	58
Plan of Rock-cut High Place above Petra . . . . . ,,	61
Court of the High Place above Petra . . . . . ,,	62
The Altar of the High Place above Petra . . . . . ,,	62
Row of Standing-stones at Gezer . . . . . . ,,	63
Elevation and Details of the Standing-stones at Gezer . . .	63
Standing-stones in a Temple at Megiddo . . . . *To face page*	65
The Rock-altar at Zar'a	66
The Northern Block of the Rock-altar at Megiddo . . *To face page*	67
Sacrificed Infant buried in a Jar . . . . . . ,,	67
Rock-surface at Megiddo, with cup-shaped depressions, and a Cave underneath	67
Jars containing the Bones of Infants found near the Corner of a Temple at Megiddo . . . . *To face page*	68
Jugs deposited in the Graves of Infants at Gezer . . . ,,	68

LIST OF ILLUSTRATIONS

Jar containing the Bones of an Infant at the Bottom of a Wall at Megiddo	70
Skeleton of a Woman found in a Hollow under the Corner of a House at Gezer . . . . *To face page*	70
Vessels from the Jar containing an Infant's Bones found at Megiddo ,,	71
Normal Lamp and Bowl Group . . . . . . ,,	72
Stamped Jar-handles	75
View of Tell Ta'annek from the North . . . . *To face page*	80
Plan of Tell Ta'annek . . . . ,,	81
Canaanite Rock-altar at Taanach	81
Two Standing-stones at Taanach . . . . *To face page*	84
Double Row of Standing-stones at Taanach . . . . ,,	84
Terra-cotta Incense-altar found at Taanach . . . . ,,	85
The Lion-seal found at Megiddo	91

MODERN RESEARCH AS ILLUSTRATING THE BIBLE

I. SKETCH OF THE PROGRESS OF RESEARCH DURING THE PAST CENTURY

The subject on which I have had the honour to be invited to address you is a large one; and in the three lectures which I have been asked to deliver it will be impossible for me to do more than call your attention to some of its more salient and important features.

The Fund is to be devoted to the furtherance of research in the archaeology, art, history, languages, and literature of Ancient Civilization with reference to Biblical Study. It will be at once apparent what a very large area is covered by these words. The object of the Trust is virtually to promote research in every department of ancient civilization that is known, for the purpose of assisting biblical study and of throwing light upon the Bible. The field is evidently a vast one: my aim to-day will be to introduce the subject by sketching in outline the course and progress of research in it during the last century.

The nineteenth century was an age of awakening—of awakening of the human mind to the value and importance of knowledge, and also to the possibility of attaining it by the use of appropriate methods. Hence the rise of an impulse to *research* in practically every department of knowledge. Need I remind any here of the enormous advances made by science during the last century? There are many sciences, of which in 1800 little or nothing was known, our knowledge of which now already fills voluminous treatises, and is continually increasing. And the same spirit of research to which these advances in the mathematical and physical sciences are due has led to similar advances in the historical sciences,—in our knowledge, for instance, of the past history of our race, of the rise and growth of civilization in different parts of the world, of the art and literature of past ages, of archaeology. And so the last century, especially the latter part of it, has been prolific with enormous discoveries relating to ancient civilization. We possessed indeed before copious and splendid monuments of the literatures of Greece and Rome and Israel; and these, though several interesting and important additions have been made to them, such as Aristotle's *Constitution of Athens*, poems of Bacchylides, the Mimes of Herodas, portions of the comedies of Menander, and extensive chapters of a Greek historian, all recovered recently from papyri,[1] have not perhaps been substantially added to: but archaeological discoveries, bearing directly upon the literatures of Greece and Rome, and indirectly upon that of Israel, have been made, of the greatest value and importance. Inscriptions, both Greek and Latin, were known before the year 1800; but since then their number has been vastly increased: Greek inscriptions from Attica, other parts of the mainland, the Aegean isles, Crete, the colonies in Asia Minor and elsewhere,[2] and Latin Inscriptions not only from Italy, but from nearly every country of Europe, as also from North Africa,[3] have thrown a flood of light upon many details of the history and antiquities of these countries. The importance of papyri has been realized only during the last thirty years, that of ostraka, or inscribed potsherds, only within the last ten years.[4] In addition to inscriptions, the excavations on the sites of ancient Troy, Mycenae, Olympia, and more recently those in Crete, which we owe to our own distinguished countryman, Dr. A. J. Evans—not to mention other places—have revealed wonderful monuments of the art and civilization which flourished in these localities, and of the character and extent of which we had before no conception. Inscriptions and such material monuments of a past civilization do not, indeed, palpitate with the life, and feeling, and

[1] See Dr. R. G. Kenyon in the *Quarterly Review*, April, 1908, pp. 333-355.

[2] The *Corpus Inscriptionum Graecarum* in four large folio volumes, edited (mainly) by Aug. Böckh (1828-59, with index by Röhl, 1877), was formerly the classical repertory of Greek Inscriptions; but that work is now superseded by the *Inscriptiones Graecae* (1873 ff.), published under the auspices of the Berlin Academy, filling now about fourteen volumes. See also, in more manageable form, Dittenberger's admirable *Sylloge Inscriptionum Graecarum* (ed. 2, 1898, 1901), *Orientis Graeci Inscriptiones Selectae* (1903, 1905), Prott and Ziehen, *Leges Graecorum Sacrae e Titulis Collectae* (1896, 1906); Collitz, *Sammlung der Griech. Dialekt-Inschriften* (vols. i-iv. 2, 1884-1905).

[3] They are collected in what Mr. (now Professor) Haverfield, in Hogarth's *Authority and Archaeology* (1899), p. 309, justly calls 'the greatest work of learning executed during the nineteenth century, the stately row of folios,' now numbering nearly forty, 'entitled the *Corpus Inscriptionum Latinarum*' (1863 ff.)—a worthy monument to the genius of the great scholar Theodor Mommsen, who planned it.

[4] See Deissmann, *New Light on the New Testament from Records of the Graeco-Roman Period* (1907), pp. 14-25.

thought, which breathe in the pages of the great poets and historians and orators of Greece and Rome, and can accordingly never form a substitute for them: but the details which they supply are of the utmost value in supplementing, supporting,—or, it may be, correcting,—and helping us to understand the great literary works of antiquity: they give us pictures of aspects of ancient life—art, religion, society, games, coinage, political and other institutions, for instance—which are only imperfectly represented in the literature which has come down to us; they often elucidate statements or allusions made by ancient writers, which but for such help from archaeology would remain more or less enigmatic; and they enable many important chapters of ancient history to be written which a hundred, or even fifty, years ago would have been out of the question.

In the case of the Bible, light has come from various quarters. Some has come from Egypt, some from the inscriptions and other monuments of the Phoenicians and other nations, who were in some cases neighbours of the Hebrews, and in all cases allied to them in race and language and civilization; but the greatest light has come from Babylonia and Assyria. Recently also excavation in Palestine has been very fruitful in yielding information about the history of the sites excavated, the peoples who successively occupied them, and the character of their civilization. And exploration in the regions visited by St. Paul, or in which there were early Jewish or Christian communities, has illustrated the archaeology, as papyri from Egypt have illustrated the language, of many parts of the New Testament. But all this also has been virtually the creation of the last century. When the nineteenth century began, many travellers in Eastern countries had indeed visited and described the principal sacred sites in Palestine; they had also in visiting Egypt or Arabia recorded observations on the customs or natural phenomena of the country, tending to illustrate allusions in the Bible; but that was all. In the study of Oriental antiquity, as in the study of classical antiquity, the nineteenth century was the period of awakening; and the progress which it witnessed is almost more than can be described. When the century began not a word of the inscriptions of either Egypt or Assyria could be read. In 1802 a Swedish Orientalist, Akerblad, succeeded in deciphering a few words in the demotic text of the trilingual Rosetta stone, which had been discovered a few years before. In the thirty years which followed, further progress was made, partly by Dr. Thomas Young, of Emmanuel College, Cambridge, but more especially by Champollion, so that by the time of the latter's death, in 1832, the decipherment

G 1*

of the Egyptian hieroglyphics was placed upon a secure basis.[1] Naturally, much remained to be done by future investigators, as indeed much even now remains to be done in the way of completing our knowledge of the language; but it is not too much to say that by the labours of a succession of brilliant explorers, the history, the art, the antiquities, the manners and customs, the domestic life of an entire civilization extending over some 4,000 years, have been disinterred and made intelligible to the present generation.[2]

A similar, only, if possible, a more wonderful story has to be told of Babylonia and Assyria. It was in the same year 1802 that Grotefend, a German classical scholar, read a few words in two cuneiform Persian texts from the rocks of Elwend, near Ḥamadān— the Achmĕtha of Ezra vi. 2, the Agbatana (Hdt. i. 98), or Ecbatana, of the classical writers—which had been copied, and published, a few years previously by the traveller, Carsten Niebuhr. Again, other scholars carried on the work thus begun; in 1846 Major (afterwards Sir Henry) Rawlinson published a complete translation of the Persian text of the long trilingual inscription of Darius on the imposing rock of Behistun, which he had climbed with great difficulty a few years before,[3] as a British officer in Persia, for the purpose of copying it.[4] Meanwhile, however, the process of excavation had begun; and M. Botta, the French vice-consul at Mosul, inspired by Julius Mohl, a pupil of the celebrated Orientalist, Silvestre de Sacy,[5] had in 1842-4 dug, with great success, into the mound of Khorsabad, twelve miles to the north, and sent a large number of sculptures and

---

[1] See further particulars in Budge, *The Mummy* (1893), pp. 124-53.

[2] See Gardner Wilkinson's *Manners and Customs of the Ancient Egyptians* (1840), ed. 2, revised and much enlarged by Samuel Birch, in three volumes, 1878, with numerous illustrations; and the more modern work of Adolf Erman, indispensable to every student of Egyptian antiquity, *Life in Ancient Egypt* (translated, 1894).

[3] See G. Rawlinson, *A Memoir of Major-General Sir H. C. Rawlinson* (1898), pp. 58, 65 f. (in 1836-7), 145 f. (in 1844). The Babylonian text, which was in a still more inaccessible part of the perpendicular front of the rock (see the illustration on the opposite page), was obtained by him in 1847, with the help of a Kurdish boy (pp. 154-7).

[4] On Grotefend, and the work of Rawlinson in reading the Persian text of this inscription, see more fully Rogers, *History of Babylonia and Assyria* (New York, 1900), i. 46-73; Evetts, *New Light on the Bible* (London, 1892), pp. 79-104; and G. Rawlinson, op. cit., pp. 56, 307-24. The names of the Persian kings were the clue with which his investigation started.

[5] Mohl had seen at the office of the East India Company in London some inscribed bricks brought from Bassorah, and was at once impressed by their importance.

The Rock of Behistun, showing the Trilingual Inscription of Darius

The rock is 1,700 feet high; and the inscription is 300 feet above its base. It is engraved upon the oblong surface shown, which also contains a representation of Darius placing his foot on a prostrate foe, while nine vanquished pretenders are led up in cords before him.

From G. Rawlinson's *Memoir of Major-General Sir H. C. Rawlinson*, p. 146.

To face p. 4]

other monuments found by him to the Louvre. The results of Botta's excavations were embodied in five magnificent folio volumes, filled with drawings and inscriptions, published by the French Government in 1849-50. In 1849 there appeared in this country a work, Mr. (afterwards Sir Henry) Layard's two volumes called *Nineveh and its Remains*, which at once produced a profound sensation. This work contained an account of excavations carried on in 1845-7 at the huge mounds of Kouyunjik (opposite to Mosul, on the left bank of the Tigris), the site of the ancient Nineveh, and of Nimrûd, eighteen miles to the south-east, the site of the ancient Calaḥ (Gen. x. 11), and of the surprising discoveries which resulted from them. Previously, as the author remarked in his Introduction, a case hardly three feet square in the British Museum contained almost all that was known to remain of both Babylon and Nineveh together. But now, palace after palace disclosed itself from under the mounds of Nimrûd and Kouyunjik; and Mr. Layard's graphic narrative told of the bas-reliefs, gigantic sculptures, paintings, and inscriptions which one after another met the astonished eyes of the explorers, and told eloquently of the varied history and civilization of a great nation which had long passed away. But as yet, except here and there by conjecture, not a word of the inscriptions found could be read. De Saulcy, in Paris, and Edw. Hincks,[1] an Irish clergyman, a man of extraordinary acumen and genius, had, however, been studying the wedge-shaped characters: Hincks as early as 1846 had read the names of Nebuchadnezzar and his father on the bricks of Babylon,[2] and by 1849 and 1850 translations had been essayed by both these men, and also by Rawlinson: but the epoch-making event of the time was the publication by Major Rawlinson in 1851 of a memoir[3] containing the Babylonian text of the Behistun inscription, with an interlinear transcription and translation, and grammatical and other notes. In this memoir the leading principles of the language—the syllabic character of the signs, and the curious and perplexing principle of *polyphony*, or the use of the same sign to express different sounds—were clearly enunciated; but it was Hincks a little later who, with his greater analytic power, established upon a firmer scientific basis both the system of writing and the grammar of Assyrian.[4] In 1853 Sir H. Layard published in his *Discoveries in*

[1] On Hincks's life and work, see an article by Canon Pooler in the *Irish Church Quarterly*, vol. i, No. 1 (1908).
[2] Layard, *Discoveries in the Ruins of Nineveh and Babylon* (1853), p. 139, *note*.
[3] Cf. G. Rawlinson, op. cit., pp. 174, 324 ff.
[4] See more fully, on the history of the decipherment of the cuneiform script

the Ruins of Nineveh and Babylon an account of a second series of excavations carried on by him in the East in 1849-51; it was a sign of the progress that had been made that in this volume translations of several inscriptions of Sennacherib and other Assyrian kings by Rawlinson and Hincks were quoted, and a list was given of Biblical names of places and persons which had been identified in the inscriptions. In the same year Mr. Hormuzd Rassam, who had formerly been Sir H. Layard's assistant, and who was now exploring independently, was fortunate enough to discover at Kouyunjik the large collection of tablets forming the library of Asshur-banipal; these were sent, as Layard's had been, to the British Museum, and proved afterwards to contain many treasures. In 1853-6 several other inscriptions were also translated by Rawlinson and others.

By all these discoveries public interest was greatly aroused; but there were still sceptics who doubted if the inscriptions had really been read. In 1857 Fox Talbot made copies of a long inscription—the annals of Tiglath-pileser I (*c*. 1100 B.C.)—which had just been published by the Trustees of the British Museum: he made his own translation, and sent it in a sealed packet to the Royal Asiatic Society; three other copies were sent to Sir Henry Rawlinson, Edw. Hincks, and Jules Oppert, of Paris; each made his translation independently; and when the four were compared they were found to agree to such an extent that it was impossible any longer to doubt that the clue to the decipherment had been found. A sure foundation had thus been gained. And since the days of Layard and Rawlinson and Hincks exploration has been busy not only at Nineveh, but also at Babylon and many other of the once populous sites in the great plain of the Tigris and the Euphrates; buildings, sculptures, and inscriptions have been disinterred in almost countless numbers; in the recesses of the British Museum, and in other museums, brick contract-tablets and other documents by the thousand are stored up —De Sarzec brought 30,000 from Telloh alone [1]—testifying to the industrial activity which existed in ancient Babylonia more than 2,000 years before Christ; hymns, epic poems, letters in great numbers, chronicles, annals of kings, paradigms and vocabularies,

(including the part taken in it by other scholars), Hommel, *Gesch. Bab. und Ass.* (1885), pp. 58-74, 90-104; Rogers, op. cit., i. 175-197; or Evetts, op. cit., pp. 105-29. Cf. also Sayce, *Archaeology of the Cuneiform Inscriptions* (1907), chap. i. Of the history of excavation in Babylonia and Assyria, the most detailed account will be found in Hilprecht's *Explorations in Bible Lands during the Nineteenth Century* (Edinb., 1903), pp. 1-577.

[1] Rogers, i. 238.

inscriptions relating to ritual, astrology, and magic, besides a very important code of laws[1], have also been discovered. A succession of gifted scholars working with these abundant materials have added enormously to the knowledge of the language which had been attained by Rawlinson and Hincks; and the civilization, including the history, the institutions, the art, and the society, of ancient Babylonia and Assyria, is now known to us in many respects more completely than that of ancient Egypt. Mr. Leonard King's *Letters and Inscriptions of Ḥammurabi*, king of Babylon in the twenty-second century B.C., contains almost as vivid a picture of life and character as do the *Life and Letters* of some statesman or prelate deceased among ourselves a few years ago. Thus the last century has witnessed what is virtually the rediscovery and reconstruction of two entire civilizations, each beginning in an almost incalculable antiquity, and each presenting a highly organized society, possessing well-developed institutions, literature, and art, and each capable of being followed, with gaps indeed in parts, but in other parts with remarkable completeness, through many centuries of a varied and eventful history. And whereas eighty years ago little was known of either nation beyond what was stated incidentally in the Old Testament or by classical writers, now voluminous works descriptive of both are being constantly written, and are quickly left behind by the progress of discovery.[2]

Although, however, the discoveries made in the countries that have been mentioned eclipse in interest almost all others, they by no means stand alone. From Phoenicia, and the Phoenician colonies; from Moab; from Palmyra and other places on the north and north-east of Palestine, once thickly covered with Aramaic-speaking populations; from districts in the north-west and south of Arabia,[3] recently also from

[1] See below, p. 26 f.

[2] It may suffice to mention here the very full account of the history and antiquities of both Egypt and Babylon contained in Maspero's three brilliantly written volumes, *The Dawn of Civilization* (ed. 4, 1901), *The Struggle of the Nations* (1896), and *The Passing of the Empires* 850 B.C. *to* 330 B.C. (1900). King and Hall's *Egypt and Western Asia in the Light of Recent Discoveries* (1907) is intended to supplement Maspero's work by giving an account of discoveries that have been made since it was completed.

[3] On the history of exploration of Arabia see Mr. Hogarth's very interesting volume *The Penetration of Arabia* (1905), with numerous plans and illustrations, and two admirable maps. The Sabaean and Minaean inscriptions of South Arabia are not at present accessible in English, nor have all that are known been as yet published. About three hundred are contained in Tom. I, fasc. 1-3 of Part iv of the *Corpus Inscriptionum Semiticarum*; and others may be expected to appear in due course. For an excellent selection of Phoenician

Elephantine, in the extreme south of Egypt,[1] inscriptions written in different Semitic dialects have been discovered, which throw valuable light on the antiquities of the countries in which they are found, and often illustrate in a most welcome manner different passages in the Old Testament. Though some of these had been copied, and were known in Europe, in the eighteenth century, very few had been read, and the great majority had not even been discovered. Gesenius, in 1837, in his *Monumenta Phoenicia*, collected, and explained with great success, the Phoenician inscriptions then known; but many additional ones, some of great interest, have been discovered since. The other inscriptions referred to have been almost entirely brought to light, and read, during the last fifty years. Most are now published in the *Corpus Inscriptionum Semiticarum*, begun at Paris in 1881, and still in course of publication: current discoveries are generally made accessible to students in the supplement to the *Corpus*, called the *Répertoire d'Épigraphie Sémitique*, and in Lidzbarski's *Ephemeris für Semitische Epigraphik*.

Nor must I omit to call special attention here to the important light thrown upon the New Testament, and the history and literature of early Christianity, by Sir W. Ramsay's long series of explorations in Asia Minor.

Some words must next be said on exploration in Palestine. Of the history of this an admirable account has been written by Dr. F. J. Bliss in his Ely Lectures on *The Development of Palestine Exploration* (1906). Many travellers have made pilgrimages to Palestine for the purpose of seeing the country, and visiting the spots consecrated by tradition, the earliest known to us being the anonymous pilgrim of Bordeaux, who made a journey to the country A.D. 333, and wrote an account of the places which he visited. Many other ancient and mediaeval pilgrims followed in his steps, and have left us their descriptions of what they saw: but the first who visited the country with a critical eye, describing minutely its physical and other features, and employing scientific methods to criticize tradition, and discriminate between proposed identifications of ancient sites, was the American Edward Robinson, whose volumes on the subject [2] laid the foundation of a scientific knowledge, both of the modern topography and of the topographical antiquities of the Holy Land. Robinson both recovered many ancient sites which had been forgotten,

---

and Aramaic inscriptions, with translations and notes, see Canon G. A. Cooke's *North-Semitic Inscriptions* (1903).   [1] See below, pp. 28-30.

[2] *Biblical Researches in Palestine and the adjacent regions: a Journal of Travels in the Years 1838 and 1852.* Ed. 2, in three volumes, 1856.

and showed the groundlessness of many identifications which had been currently accepted. Since Robinson's day the work has been continued partly by individual explorers—such as Trumbull, for instance, who rediscovered and fixed the site of Kadesh-barnea—and by societies, among which a leading place is taken by the English Palestine Exploration Fund, founded in 1865, and the German Palästina-Verein, established in 1877. It was under the auspices of the former that underground Jerusalem was explored by Sir Charles Warren in 1867-8, and a survey of Western Palestine made, on a scale of an inch to the mile, by Capt. Stewart, Capt. (now Col.) Conder, and Capt. (now Lord) Kitchener, in 1871-8, the map, with memoirs describing the topography, antiquities, and flora and fauna of the country, being published shortly afterwards. As a key to the topography of Palestine, the inch to the mile map of the country west of Jordan, published by the Palestine Exploration Fund, is beyond all praise, and of the utmost value to the serious Bible student, who can realize with its help the historical significance of mountains and hills, passes and streams, and, where the sites are sufficiently certain,[1] can follow upon it the movements of a Barak or a Gideon, a Samson or a David, up and down a hill-side, or elsewhere, with the greatest ease. In the autumn of 1868 and winter of 1869, also, a very thorough survey was made by Capt. (afterwards Major) H. S. Palmer, and Capt. (afterwards Sir C. W.) Wilson, of the Sinaitic Peninsula, a detailed account of which, with maps, descriptions, and photographs, was published in 1872 in five folio volumes. The results of all these explorations and surveys were summed up, in their bearing upon the history of Israel, by Dean Stanley (as far as they had been then reached) in 1856, and by George Adam Smith

[1] A most important proviso to remember. The inch-to-the-mile map of the Palestine Exploration Fund contains only the names of modern sites; the 'Old and New Testament Map of Palestine,' in twenty sheets, on the scale of $\frac{3}{8}$ of an inch to the mile, includes ancient sites as well, sites doubtfully identified (of which there are a good many—some very improbable) being distinguished by queries. Unfortunately, however, in current maps of Palestine the identifications of the Palestine Exploration Fund are often reproduced *without the queries*: hence, in using such maps, the student who does not desire to be misled must always, in the case of any less well-known site, satisfy himself, by consulting a good commentary or biblical dictionary, that the grounds for the identification are sufficient. The map of Palestine in Murray's *Handy Classical Maps*, though convenient and useful in showing the elevations, is often at fault in this respect; but questionable identifications have by some means found their way even into the maps edited by G. A. Smith. A critical map of Palestine, including ancient sites, on a convenient scale is a *desideratum* at present.

in 1894.¹ But valuable as the work of these explorers was, it dealt, except in the case of that of Capt. Warren, exclusively with the *surface* of Palestine. A new epoch was inaugurated in the history of Palestine exploration, when in 1890, Prof. Flinders Petrie, bringing to bear upon Palestine the experience he had gained in Egypt, began to explore Palestine *below* the surface, and started by digging into the lofty mound of Tell el-Ḥesy, in the south-west of Judah. Here systematic excavation, scientifically conducted, revealed the *débris* of eleven cities,² superposed in strata one above another, extending, as pottery and other articles found in them showed, from something like 1700 B.C. to 400 B.C. The success attending the exploration of Tell el-Ḥesy soon stimulated other explorers to begin work upon promising sites elsewhere. Dr. Bliss, who continued the work at Tell el-Ḥesy begun by Prof. Petrie, in 1898 commenced work with Mr. Macalister at Tell eṣ-Ṣāfi, probably Gath, and shortly afterwards at Tell Zakariya, Tell ej-Judeideh, and Tell Sandaḥannah, all in the south-west of Judah. In 1902, Mr. Macalister began the excavation of Gezer, seventeen miles north-west of Jerusalem, which is still (1908) continuing. In the same year (Mar. 10-July 12) Prof. Sellin of Vienna, with the assistance partly of the Austrian Government and the Vienna Academy of Inscriptions, and partly of private donors, began excavations at Taanach, in the plain of Esdraelon, in the north of Palestine, which were resumed for three weeks in 1903 (March 7-30), and again for nearly four weeks (Aug. 6-Sept. 2) in 1904;³ and in 1903-5⁴ Dr. Schumacher, at the instance of the German Palestine Society, was working similarly at the neighbouring Tell el-Mutesellim, the site, in all probability, of the ancient Megiddo. All these excavations have been most fruitful in yielding results respecting the history of the sites in question, and the civilization and other characteristics of the peoples who successively built cities upon them, of which I hope to give some particulars in subsequent lectures. At the present moment (March, 1908), Dr. Sellin is engaged in the ex-

¹ See the note on p. 31.
² Bliss, *A Mound of Many Cities* (1894), Plate II, pp. 14, 123.
³ See Sellin, *Tell Taʻannek*, with plans and numerous illustrations (Vienna, 1904), from the *Denkschriften* of the Vienna Academy (Phil.-Hist. Klasse), vol. 1, part 4; and *Eine Nachlese auf dem Tell Taʻannek* (Vienna, 1905)—describing the excavations of 1904—from vol. lii, part 3, of the same *Denkschriften*.
⁴ See the provisional reports in the *Mitteilungen und Nachrichten des Deutschen Palästina-Vereins*, 1904, p. 14 ff.-1906, p. 65 ff. Since these lectures were delivered vol. i of the full report, containing nearly 300 illustrations, and accompanied by fifty plates of plans, and illustrations of the objects found, has been issued, edited by Prof. Steuernagel (*Tell el-Mutesellim*, Leipzig, 1908).

cavation of the large mound which marks the site of the ancient Jericho; and Dr. Schumacher, at the invitation of Harvard University, is about to begin the excavation of Samaria; from both of which, judging by the experience of other places, much may be hoped.

Let me now turn for a few moments to the languages of antiquity, to the investigation of which our Trust offers its help. The languages in which the Bible is written—Hebrew, Aramaic, and Greek—are all, virtually, dead languages; and the text of the Bible has come down to us in manuscripts, none—except a few fragments—older than the fourth century of our era, and, of the Hebrew MSS., none older than the ninth or tenth century A.D. Texts handed down in this way from ancient times are all liable to corruption in the process of transcription; and the MSS. of the Bible form no exception to the rule. In the New Testament the MSS. themselves differ constantly from each other—mostly, indeed, in unimportant particulars, but sometimes upon important points; and there are cases in which a decision as to which of two variant readings is the original is very difficult. In the Old Testament the MSS., though they do differ, do not differ as often or as widely as those of the New Testament; but this is due, not to the fact that the text which they preserve is purer, but in all probability to the fact that they are descended from a single archetype, separated by a considerable interval of time from the original autographs; and when the text in which they agree is examined closely, it becomes only too apparent that it contains numerous corruptions. Fortunately many of these can be corrected by the testimony of the Ancient Versions—which are many centuries earlier in date than any Hebrew MSS., and were in many cases made from Hebrew MSS. which were still free from these corruptions; but others, if they can be removed at all, can be removed only by conjecture.[1] The study of the Ancient Versions, including the determination of their texts, is one of the most valuable auxiliaries of biblical research. The improvements which they enable scholars to make in the Hebrew Bible are often illuminating; and

[1] Of course, conjecture in reason and moderation; for there can be no doubt that some writers are far too ready with this potent but perilous restorative. As Dr. Kenyon has shown in a very important paper on 'The Evidence of Greek Papyri with regard to Textual Criticism' (published in the *Proceedings of the British Academy*, 1903–4, pp. 139 ff.), the papyri of classical texts confirm the emendations of editors only to a limited extent. Hebrew texts, from the character of the script, are, it is true, more liable to corruption than Greek texts, and the Ancient Versions afford convincing evidence that the Old Testament has in very many places been corrupted seriously; still, the parallel suggests caution.

are apparent, if they are placed before him clearly, to any intelligent reader. Examples will be found noted on the margin of the Revised Version, though the number might readily be increased. Let us, however, suppose that, with the help of all these aids, we have got the text of the Bible as pure as possible; there are still difficulties to be surmounted. The languages in which it was written are, as has been said, virtually dead; and in dealing with any literature of this kind the modern interpreter often finds himself pulled up. No one can quite gain the same mastery over a dead language that he can gain over a living one. He does not move entirely in the same circle of ideas as those who spoke the language; he has not that instinctive knowledge of the force of a word, a phrase, an allusion, which was possessed by those who moved among the circumstances to which its writers refer: by long study, and sometimes laborious research, he can more or less successfully place himself in that position; and the great masters of ancient language have done that: but he still finds words, and phrases, and allusions which remain uncertain and obscure, and the uncertainty is sometimes the greater because he does not feel sure that the text is in its original form. Hence the need of *philology*, and the study of a language grammatically and lexically, which often combines with the knowledge of material facts conveyed by archaeology to illuminate a passage of an ancient writer. A hundred years ago our knowledge of the biblical languages was very much less than it is now. Even for classical Greek there was not a decent Greek-English lexicon. The first edition of Liddell and Scott's Greek Lexicon—scarcely half the size of the last—appeared in 1843. Commentaries, though there were some of exhaustive learning, showed too often a lack of the historical sense, and were insufficient. But during the last century an immense amount of labour has been spent by the ablest hands upon the languages of the Bible. Both grammar and lexicon have been minutely and comprehensively studied with all the aids that the fuller knowledge, and the more scientific methods, of the nineteenth century could supply. For the elucidation of Hebrew in particular, a new science, unknown to our forefathers, sprang up, the science of comparative philology. The mediaeval Jews, many of whom were familiar with Arabic, were naturally aware that Arabic, and also Aramaic, were allied to Hebrew; and not unfrequently appealed to Arabic and Aramaic in determining the sense of some rare word in the Old Testament. They had, however, no idea of an organic connexion between the different languages of the Semitic family, with definite rules regulating the interchange of sounds between them, any more than the older classical scholars had any idea how what are now called the Indo-European languages (i.e. Greek, Latin, and their cognates) were all organically connected. This last discovery was first made in the early years of the nineteenth century, when Sanskrit, which was then making itself known among the scholars of Europe, suddenly threw a flood of light upon the organic connexion subsisting between these languages. And the discovery of Sanskrit gave such a shock to current prepossessions that in 1824-5 an eminent Scotch philosopher, Dugald Stewart, wrote an essay in which he endeavoured to show that it was an artificial language, concocted by the Brahmans upon the basis of Greek, of which a knowledge had reached them through the conquests of Alexander the Great.[1] For the Semitic languages, the same relationship was first established by a Spanish Jesuit named Hervas, who in 1800 drew up tables of the declensions and conjugations in Hebrew, Aramaic, Arabic, Ethiopic, and Amharic, making it evident that all these languages were dialects of one original language, and consequently that all belonged to the same family.[2] Assyrian was not yet known: when its forms were discovered, it quickly appeared that it was also a member of the same group. In the further study of the subject it soon became evident that Arabic was an older language than Hebrew, and by preserving more original forms threw most light upon the comparative philology of the entire family—a pre-eminence which it was found afterwards had partly to be shared with it by Assyrian. But Hebrew being thus one of a number of related languages, the importance of these other languages in their bearing upon Hebrew becomes apparent. They frequently elucidate points of philology or lexicography which, if we had Hebrew alone to guide us, would remain obscure. If we had only English to guide us, how could we discover the meaning of 'worth' in the phrase 'Woe worth the day,' which occurs both in the English Bible (Ezek. xxx. 2), and in a well-known line of Sir Walter Scott? German tells us the meaning at once;[3] and Arabic often performs a similar service for Hebrew. It would be easy to quote examples of words occurring in the Old Testament, which have been elucidated by Assyrian or other

---

[1] *Works* (ed. Sir Wm. Hamilton), iv. 115, *note*. A long section of vol. iii of his *Elements of the Philosophy of the Human Mind* (1827) was devoted by him to the same subject (ibid., pp. 77-115). The essay was never published.

[2] See Max Müller's *Lectures on the Science of Language*, first series, ed. 1861, p. 141.

[3] 'Worth' = *become* (γένοιτο), Germ. *werde* (from *werden*, 'to become'), A.S. *weorð*: so 'Woe worth' means 'Woe betide.' See Aldis Wright's *Bible Word-Book*, s. v. *Woe worth*, where numerous examples from old writers are cited.

inscriptions.[1] And we never know antecedently what word or expression may not be illustrated or explained by a newly discovered inscription. Examples have occurred within the last year or two. Hence the importance of exploration for the purpose, if possible, of discovering new inscriptions; for one of these may at any moment throw unexpected light upon something in the Bible.

Before leaving this branch of my subject, I may make a few remarks on the language of the New Testament. Our knowledge of biblical Greek, like that of classical Greek, has advanced during the last century from the more careful study of the relevant facts, and from the application of more exact philological and grammatical investigation. But, almost within the last decade, important fresh light has been thrown upon biblical Greek from inscriptions and papyri, especially the latter, which, at first chiefly through the researches of Prof. Petrie, and more recently through the indefatigable labours of Drs. Grenfell and Hunt,[2] have now been made accessible in great numbers. These papyri have yielded an immense amount of information on the political administration and social life of Egypt under the Ptolemies; but beyond that they have shown that biblical Greek, if by that term is meant the idiom of the Septuagint and of the New Testament to the exclusion of other Greek, is a misnomer; that this idiom, except in so far as it contains pure Hebraisms, has nothing distinctive about it, and that it is simply the colloquial Greek that was spoken at the time when the books in question were written. Other contemporary inscriptions—the numerous ones found at Pergamum, for instance—have confirmed this conclusion. The old antithesis of biblical and profane Greek in the sense in which it used to be understood is thus seen now to be incorrect; many words formerly described as peculiar to biblical Greek being now found, as Prof. Deissmann especially has shown,[3] in papyri and Greek inscriptions, dating from the centuries shortly before and after Christ. To take but one example: the extant parts of the great sacrificial calendar of Cos, published by

---

[1] See examples (which might be readily added to) in the writer's essay in Hogarth's *Authority and Archaeology* (1899), pp. 131-42.

[2] See also the three large volumes of *Greek Papyri in the British Museum*, edited by Dr. Kenyon (1893, 1898, 1907).

[3] See examples in his *Bible Studies* (translated, Edinburgh, 1901, ed. 2, 1903): comp. also his *New Light on the New Testament* (1903), *The Philology of the Greek Bible* (1908), and, on a more comprehensive scale, with facsimiles of inscriptions, &c., his *Licht vom Osten: Das N.T. und die neuentdeckten Texte der hellenistisch-römischen Welt* (1908).

Canon Hicks in 1888,[1] both offers a curious parallel to some of the regulations in Leviticus, and illustrates some rather remarkable sacrificial terms (καρπόω, κάρπωσις, κάρπωμα) used in the LXX. Already grammars to the Greek of both the Septuagint and the New Testament, embodying the new knowledge, have begun to appear[2]; and probably the next few years will see the compilation of new lexicons to both these branches of biblical Greek, in which the fresh light thus thrown upon many of the words used in biblical Greek will similarly be utilized.[3]

I hope that this survey, rapid and imperfect as it necessarily has been, may be sufficient to show how actively research, such as may be broadly described in one word as archaeological, has been recently, and still is being, carried on; and how much light it has thrown, in one way or another, upon the history and antiquities of Palestine and neighbouring countries, and so sometimes directly, sometimes indirectly, upon the archaeology and philology of the Bible. In the rest of these lectures, I shall make it my endeavour to place before you some concrete examples, which may both illustrate the importance of these studies and awaken interest in them. Meanwhile, it may be worth while remarking that one outstanding result of the studies and researches which I have been thus rapidly reviewing has been to take the Hebrews out of the isolated position which, as a nation, they seemed previously to hold, and to demonstrate their affinities with, and often their dependence upon, the civilizations by which they were surrounded. Tribes more or less closely akin to themselves in both language and race were their neighbours on the north, east, and south: in addition to this, on each side there towered above them an ancient and imposing civilization, that of Babylonia, from the earliest times active, enterprising, and full of life, and that of Egypt, hardly, if at all, less remarkable than that of Babylonia, though more self-contained, and exerting less influence on foreign countries. It was Babylonia which, as we now know, exercised in ancient times an influence over Western Asia, once entirely unsuspected. Palestine itself, as the Tell el-Amarna letters show, must have been for some centuries before it fell into the power of Egypt, at about 1500 B.C., a province of Babylonia, in which at least

---

[1] *Journal of Hellenic Studies*, ix. 324-37 (= Paton and Hicks, *The Inscriptions of Cos*, 1891, pp. 77-94).

[2] Helbing, *Grammatik der Septuaginta* (Laut- und Wortlehre), 1907; J. H. Moulton, *A Grammar of New Testament Greek*, vol. i (1906).

[3] See Moulton's series of 'Lexical Notes from the Papyri' in the *Expositor* for 1904, resumed, ibid. Jan., Feb., March, July, Aug., Sept., Oct., 1908.

by the official classes the language and cuneiform script of Babylonia were used: some of the early narratives of Genesis point unmistakably to Babylonia as their source; and recent discoveries have given indications that even in later times the strong arm of Assyria was felt in Palestine more than the biblical records would imply. Undoubtedly in some quarters the influence of Babylon upon Israel has been exaggerated; but the last thirty years have certainly shown that it was both real and considerable. These affinities between Israel and its neighbours must not, however, be misunderstood. They do not detract from that unique religious pre-eminence which has always been deemed an inalienable characteristic of the Hebrew race; but the secular institutions of the nation, and even the material elements upon which the religious system of the Israelites was constructed, are seen now to have been in many cases common to them with their neighbours. Thus their beliefs about the origin and early history of the world, their social usages, their code of civil and criminal law, their religious institutions, can no longer be viewed, as was once possible, as differing in kind from those of other nations, and determined in every detail by a direct revelation from Heaven: all, it is now known, have substantial analogies among other peoples—the distinctive character which they exhibit among the Hebrews consisting in the spirit with which they are infused, and the deep religious truths of which they are made the exponents.

All that I can do in the rest of to-day's lecture is to illustrate what I have said by glancing at some of the more interesting and important discoveries of the last sixty years in their bearing upon the Bible.[1] I must, however, premise that the really important and valuable archaeological discoveries are not those which merely corroborate isolated biblical statements, the correctness of which has never been challenged; but those which rectify or supplement the biblical statements, and especially those which enable us to form a picture of the history and civilization of the East as a whole and of the place taken by Israel in it, and of the nature of the influences which, as we now see, it exerted upon Israel. One of the first achievements of Assyriology was the translation of the inscription on the celebrated Black Obelisk, sent to London by Layard in 1846, and now a conspicuous object in the British Museum. The upper

---

[1] For further particulars respecting several of the discoveries here noticed, and also for some account of many not noticed here at all, see the writer's essay in Hogarth's *Authority and Archaeology* (1899), pp. 1–152. Those mentioned here are arranged in such a way as to illustrate the *progress* of discovery.

The Black Obelisk of Shalmaneser II
The second tier from the top represents the tribute of Jehu.
From Stade's *Geschichte des Volkes Israel*, i (1887), p. 563.

The Tribute of Jehu as represented on the Black Obelisk
From Stade's *Geschichte des Volkes Israel*, i. 564, 565.

To face p. 17]

part of this obelisk consists of five tiers of bas-reliefs, representing tribute brought by subject nations to the Assyrian king: the apex and lower part are occupied by the inscription. This inscription proved to be the annals of Shalmaneser II (860-825 B.C.). It was the first long inscription read by Rawlinson;[1] and he read it, in the main correctly,[2] in 1850 : but Hincks, in 1851, first read in the superscription over one of the bas-reliefs the name of Jehu, king of Israel, as that of one of the tributary kings.[3] The words are—

Tribute of Jehu, of the house of Ḥumri[4] (Omri) : silver, gold, a golden bowl, a golden ladle, golden goblets, golden pitchers, lead, a staff for the hand of the king, (and) bdellium, I received.

The tribute-bearers are bearded, and have a strongly marked Jewish physiognomy. 'The $^{(land)}$ House of Omri[5]' is the standing name for the Northern Kingdom in the Assyrian inscriptions. The same inscription, as both Hincks and Rawlinson[6] shortly afterwards independently discovered, mentions also how Shalmaneser defeated Hazael, king of Damascus, the general who (2 Kings viii. 15) smothered Benhadad to death, and then seized the throne.

In 1852 (*Athenaeum*, Jan. 3, p. 26), Hincks read the name of Menahem of Samaria as paying tribute in the eighth year of a king's reign, afterwards found to be Tiglath-Pileser III (745-727 B.C.); and in 1853 (*Athenaeum*, Feb. 18, 1854, p. 216), Rawlinson found at Nimrûd a list of eighteen monarchs subject to the same king, including Rezin of Damascus, Menahem of Samaria, and Hiram of Tyre.

Other inscriptions relating to the same period of the history have since come to light. The Book of Kings (2 Kings xv. 29, 30) mentions that in the reign of Pekah, Tiglath-Pileser took various districts in the north and east of Israel, and carried their inhabitants into exile, and adds that Hoshea conspired against Pekah, and slew

---

[1] *Journal of the Royal Asiatic Society*, xii. 431-48. Cf. Hommel, *Gesch. Bab. und Ass.*, p. 92 ; Sayce, *Archaeology of the Cuneiform Inscriptions* (1907), p. 20 f.

[2] He chiefly went astray in the proper names, for which the uncertainty of many of the characters was a sufficient excuse.

[3] *Athenaeum*, Dec. 27, 1851, p. 1384 f. Rawlinson soon afterwards read the same name independently (ibid., March 27, 1852, p. 357). In the *Journal of the Royal As. Soc.*, p. 447, he had read the name as 'Yahua, son of Ḥubiri,' and did not recognize who was meant.

[4] Commonly rendered 'son of Ḥumri', and supposed to be an error on the part of the Assyrian king. But Ungnad has shown recently (*Orient. Litt.-Zeit.*, 1906, p. 225 f.) that the rendering given above is quite legitimate.

[5] The sign rendered $^{(land)}$ is a determinative prefix, indicating a country.

[6] *Athenaeum*, Dec. 27, 1851, and March 27, 1852, p. 357.

him, and reigned in his stead. In Tiglath-Pileser's annals, first brought to light (see below) by Mr. George Smith in 1867, we read, 'The (land of the) House of Omri (i.e. the Northern Kingdom), the whole of its inhabitants, together with their possessions, to Assyria I deported. Pekah, their king, I slew; Hoshea to rule over them I appointed. Ten talents of gold, 1,000 talents of silver, I received from them.' The 'whole' of the inhabitants must be an exaggeration; but in other respects the inscription agrees with the biblical statement; and we learn from it the additional fact that the conspiracy in Samaria, which cost Pekah his throne and life, was carried through with the help of Assyria: 'Pekah, their king, I slew; Hoshea to rule over them I appointed.' We knew before (2 Kings xv. 19) that Menahem had been supported on his throne by Tiglath-Pileser;[1] but we did not know before that Hoshea owed his crown to him as well.

Sargon (722-705) is mentioned in the Old Testament only once, incidentally (Isa. xx. 1), as besieging Ashdod, and so affording the occasion for a short prophecy of Isaiah's. From his annals we learn that his reign was an eventful one, full of military achievements, and that it lasted for seventeen years. The revolt of Ashdod, which led to the siege mentioned by Isaiah, took place in his eleventh year.[2] But, as Rawlinson was able to point out in 1851,[3] he gives us more interesting information than this. From the Book of Kings[4] we should suppose that it was Shalmaneser who, after a three years' siege, took Samaria, and carried Israel into exile in Assyria; but from the annals of Sargon we learn that this was not the case: the capture of Samaria was one of the first successes of Sargon's reign, and he gives us particulars about it:—

The city of Samaria I besieged, I took; . . . 27,290 of its inhabitants I carried into captivity; fifty of their chariots I seized . . . ; people from all lands, my captives, I settled there; my officers I appointed governors over them; tribute and dues I exacted of them.[5]

---

[1] In 2 Kings xv. 19 'Pul'. The identity of Pul with Tiglath-Pileser had been strongly suspected before; it was made a certainty by a dynastic list containing the name, which was found by Mr. Pinches in the British Museum, and published by him in 1884.

[2] *Annals*, ll. 208, 224 f.

[3] *Athenaeum*, Aug. 23, 1851, p. 903. Rawlinson cites from the transcript, given in Plate 70 of Botta's great work, of the Annals of Sargon, inscribed on the walls of the palace at Khorsabad. See Winckler's *Die Keilschrifttexte Sargons*, vol. i (1889), p. 5, ll. 10-17, and the duplicate in the 'Prunkinschrift,' ibid., p. 101, ll. 23-5.

[4] 2 Kings xvii. 3, 6.   [5] Winckler, p. 5; cf. p. 101, also pp. 83, 149.

INSCRIPTIONS NAMING ISRAELITE KINGS

The statement that people from other places were settled by Sargon in Samaria agrees with 2 Kings xvii. 24.

Sargon's successor on the throne was Sennacherib (705-681). The reading of the famous inscription of Sennacherib, which mentions Hezekiah, also takes us back to the early years of Assyrian study in England. Dr. Hincks, in 1849,[1] was the first to detect the name of Sennacherib at the beginning of nearly all the inscriptions, and on all the inscribed bricks, brought from the great palace at Kouyunjik; but the account of the campaign in which Sennacherib invaded Judah was first read by Rawlinson in 1851 from the copy taken by Layard of an inscription on one of the colossal bulls which guarded the grand entrance to the palace.[2] The entire inscription, embracing the first six years of Sennacherib's reign, was shortly afterwards translated independently by Dr. Hincks.[3] This inscription fixes the date of the invasion of Judah mentioned in 2 Kings xviii to Sennacherib's third year (701 B.C.): we learn further from the inscription, what would not have been suspected from the biblical narrative, that Hezekiah's revolt was part of a concerted plan of rebellion, in which many of the cities of Phoenicia and the Philistines took part; and that Sennacherib's invasion of Judah was but an episode in a campaign undertaken by him for the purpose of suppressing this general scheme of revolt. Accordingly, he tells us first how he invaded Phoenicia, and reduced Zidon and other cities; then how he received the homage of several neighbouring kings—the kings of Ashdod, Ammon, Moab, and Edom for instance; then how he advanced into the Philistine country, south-west of Judah, reduced the cities there which had revolted, and defeated the Egyptians who came to their aid—we remember how the Rabshakeh taunts Hezekiah with trusting in the 'broken reed', Egypt—and then, lastly, proceeded to attack Judah:

And Hezekiah of Judah, who had not submitted to my yoke, forty-six of his strong cities, fortresses and smaller towns without number, I besieged, I took; 200,150 people, horses, mules, asses, camels, oxen, and sheep without number, from the midst of them I brought out, I counted them as spoil. Himself, as a bird in a cage, in Jerusalem, his royal city, I shut up. Siege-works against him I constructed; and those coming out of the gate of his city I turned back.

His cities, Sennacherib continues, he gave to the Philistine kings who had remained loyal to Assyria. He imposed tribute upon

---

[1] Layard, *Discoveries in Nineveh and Babylon* (1853), p. 139.
[2] *Athenaeum*, Aug. 23, 1851.
[3] Layard, op. cit., p. 139. See the full account of its contents, pp. 139-44.

Hezekiah, and directed an immense amount of valuables from Jerusalem to be sent after him to Nineveh. With these particulars his narrative of the campaign closes. Sennacherib is silent with regard to the great pestilence which, according to the Book of Kings, caused so many of his soldiers to perish; but neither, it may be noticed, does he claim to have taken Jerusalem.

I wish I had time to show in detail what light the contemporary Assyrian inscriptions throw upon many passages in the prophecies of Isaiah, and how they enable us to understand the movements of political parties in Israel and Judah, and the attitude adopted towards them by Isaiah.[1]

In the same year (1851) Hincks explained the term 'Tartan' (Isa. xx. 1, 2 Kings xviii. 17) as being the Assyrian word for 'general', found more than once in Sargon's inscriptions.

The Second Book of Kings makes an interval of eight years between the capture of Samaria by Sargon and Sennacherib's expedition against Hezekiah (2 Kings xviii. 10, 13). Rawlinson had noted in 1851 that,[2] according to his annals found at Khorsabad, Sargon had reigned at least fifteen years; so that, as Sennacherib's expedition was fixed by the bull-inscription to his third year, there must have been at least eighteen years between the two events; and Hincks in 1852[3] was able to announce definitely, and almost correctly, that Sargon began to reign in 721 and Sennacherib in 703 B.C. At first it was thought that the biblical dates could be adjusted to the Assyrian by the simple supposition of a clerical error in the biblical text; but as the annals of the Assyrian kings became more completely known, and especially after Sir H. Rawlinson in 1862 discovered texts of the 'Eponym Canon,' giving the eponymous officers of each year from 909 to 647 B.C.[4], it became clear that this explanation was not sufficient: there were other discrepancies between the biblical and Assyrian dates which could not be explained as due merely to textual corruption;[5] and the conclusion of literary criticism was confirmed that the chronological system of the Book

---

[1] See *Isaiah, his Life and Times*, by the present writer, in the 'Men of the Bible' series.

[2] *Athenaeum*, Aug. 23, 1851, p. 903.

[3] *Athenaeum*, Sept. 14, 1852, p. 984.

[4] See G. Smith's *Assyrian Eponym Canon*, pp. 27 ff.

[5] Ahab, for instance, according to Ussher's computation of the dates in the Book of Kings, reigned 918-897 B.C.; but in an inscription of Shalmaneser II he is mentioned at a date equivalent to 854 B.C. See the writer's *Isaiah, his Life and Times*, pp. 12-14.

of Kings is not part of the original documents preserved in them, but is the work of the compiler, who arrived at it by computation from the regnal years of the successive kings known to him, the errors in it being due either to the *data* at his disposal, or to his calculations, being in some cases incorrect.

Sennacherib was succeeded by Esarhaddon (681-668), and Esarhaddon by Asshurbanipal (668-625). Both these kings mention Manasseh as paying tribute. Asshurbanipal also gives an account of his invasion of Egypt and capture of Thebes, which explains the allusion in Nah. iii. 8, and also gives a *terminus a quo* (663 B.C.) for fixing the date of Nahum's prophecy.

In 1868 a most valuable discovery was made in another quarter. In 2 Kings iii. 4, 5, we read that Mesha, king of Moab, was a sheepmaster, who paid the king of Israel a large annual tribute in wool, but that after the death of Ahab he rebelled. In 1868 there was found accidentally at Dibon on the east of the Dead Sea, in the territory of the ancient Moab, a large slab of black basalt, bearing an inscription, which proved to contain Mesha's own account of the circumstances of the revolt. It was first edited in this country in 1871, with valuable notes, by Dr. Ginsburg. Omri, we learn from it, had gained possession of many of the cities claimed by Moab; and Mesha describes how he recovered them for Moab, and rebuilt and fortified them in the event of a siege. Most of the places named are mentioned in the Old Testament in descriptions of the territory on the east of Jordan. In one, Nebo, there was a sanctuary of Jehovah: Mesha took it by assault, robbed it of its sacred vessels, and dragged them in triumph before Chemosh, the national god of Moab. The inscription furnishes many most interesting illustrations of the language and ideas of the Old Testament. The language differs only dialectically from Hebrew; and in style it reads like a chapter from the Book of Judges or Kings. The terms in which Chemosh is spoken of are singularly like those used of Jehovah in the Old Testament. Chemosh is 'angry' with his people, just as Jehovah sometimes is with Israel: he says to Mesha, 'Go, take Nebo,' or 'Go down, fight against Ḥoronên'—just as we read, for instance (1 Sam. xxiii. 4), 'Arise, go down to Keilah,' or (2 Sam. xxiv. 1), 'Go, number Israel and Judah'; and he 'drives out' Mesha's foes before him, just as Jehovah 'drives out' the foes of Israel (Josh. xxiv. 18). And Mesha 'devotes' the inhabitants of a captured city to his god, just as in the Book of Joshua and elsewhere we often read of the Israelites doing (e. g. Josh. vi. 21 R. V. *marg.*; 1 Sam. xv. 3, 15 R.V. *marg.*). The inscription of Mesha comes nearer to the Old

Testament, and illustrates it more directly, than any other inscription hitherto found.[1] Excavation in Moab in quest of other ancient Moabite inscriptions would be well worth instituting.

Let us return, however, to the inscriptions of Assyria and Babylonia. In 1866, a young man, George Smith by name, originally designed for an engraver, inspired by what he had read of the discoveries of Layard and Rawlinson, was fired with a desire to prosecute research upon the same field himself. He accordingly obtained permission from Sir H. Rawlinson to examine some of the inscriptions which, often in a fragmentary form, had by this time begun to accumulate in great numbers in the British Museum. Before long he found a fragment of an inscription[2] which fixed the date of the tribute of Jehu to Shalmaneser mentioned on the Black Obelisk to that king's eighteenth year. After this proof of his ability, he was chosen to assist Sir H. Rawlinson in preparing for publication vol. iii of his *Cuneiform Inscriptions of Western Asia*; and shortly afterwards discovered in the annals of Tiglath-Pileser II in the Museum the notices respecting Pekah and Hoshea, already quoted (p. 18). George Smith had a rare talent both for recognizing cuneiform signs and for piecing together broken tablets; and, pursuing his studies, published in 1871 a full text of the annals of Asshurbanipal. In 1872 he had the good fortune, while working upon some of the clay tablets brought by Rassam from the library of Asshurbanipal, to find some fragments which manifestly contained parallels to the biblical story of the Deluge. On Dec. 3, 1872, George Smith read a paper on his discovery before the Society of Biblical Archaeology. It aroused, as was to be expected, great interest; and the proprietors of the *Daily Telegraph*, moved by the editor, Edwin Arnold, offered George Smith a thousand guineas if he would go to Nineveh, explore for himself, and describe his discoveries in their paper. He went; and, not to dwell here upon other discoveries, found, on May 14, 1873, in the same room of Asshurbanipal's palace in which the previous fragments had been discovered, a new fragment, which fitted into the previous ones. Not long afterwards he discovered tablets containing parts of the Babylonian account of the Creation.[3] Both the Creation and the Deluge Tablets, together with

---

[1] A full translation of it will be found in Hogarth's *Authority and Archaeology*, p. 89 f.; also in Hastings's *Dict. of the Bible*, iii, s.v. MOAB; or in the *Encyclopaedia Biblica*, iii, s.v. MESHA.

[2] Translated in Schrader's *Keilinschriftliche Bibliothek*, i (1889), p. 141 (footnote).

[3] *Assyrian Discoveries* (1875), pp. 97, 102; *Chaldaean Genesis*, pp. 6 ff.

other mythological texts, were published by him in 1876 in his *Chaldaean Account of Genesis*. On his return from a third visit to the East, in 1876, he died of fever, to the great loss of science, and to the deep regret of all interested in the progress of Assyriology, at Aleppo.

The Creation and Deluge Tablets are important. The former describe, in mythological form, the triumph of Marduk, the supreme god of Babylon—the Merodach of Jer. l. 2—over the powers of confusion and disorder, and his gradual creation of an ordered world. They have been edited most recently, with additional parts that have been discovered since George Smith's death (including one describing Marduk's creation of man), by Mr. Leonard King in his *Seven Tablets of Creation* (1902) [vol. i, transliteration and translation; vol. ii, cuneiform texts].[1] The Deluge Tablets form the eleventh canto of an epic poem narrating the exploits of Gilgamesh, the hero of Uruk (the Erech of Gen. x. 10), and very possibly, though at present the supposition is not more than a conjecture, the biblical Nimrod (Gen. x. 8–11, Mic. v. 6). Gilgamesh's ancestor, Ut-na-pishtim, it was said, had received the gift of immortality; and Gilgamesh, anxious to learn the secret by which he had obtained this boon, crosses the Waters of Death to visit and question him. Ut-napishtim in reply tells him that, when the gods had determined to destroy Shurippak, a city on the Euphrates, by means of a flood, he had, on account of his piety, been warned by Ea, and counselled to save himself by building a great ship; after the flood had subsided, and he had quitted his ark, he had been endowed by Bel with immortality.[2] The Babylonian narratives are both polytheistic, while the corresponding biblical narratives (Gen. i and vi–ix) are made the vehicle of a pure and exalted monotheism; but in spite of this fundamental difference, and also variations in detail, the resemblances are such as to leave no doubt that the Hebrew cosmogony and the Hebrew story of the Deluge are both derived ultimately from the same original as the Babylonian narratives, only transformed by the magic touch of Israel's religion, and infused by it with a new spirit.

In 1877 inscriptions from Ephesus, published by Mr. J. T. Wood, illustrated in a most welcome manner the narrative in Acts xix. 23 ff.

---

[1] See excerpts also in the present writer's *Book of Genesis* (ed. 5, 1906), pp. 28 ff.
[2] The entire narrative is translated in C. J. Ball's *Light from the East* (1899), pp. 35 ff.; for excerpts illustrating the biblical descriptions, see *Authority and Archaeology*, pp. 23 ff., or the writer's *Genesis*, pp. 104 ff.

of the disturbance caused in Ephesus by St. Paul's preaching there, and of the tumultuous meeting in the theatre. A decree of the people of Ephesus, published long before by Boeckh,[1] had, indeed, witnessed eloquently to the wide diffusion of the worship of the Ephesian Artemis, and the pride which the city felt in maintaining it worthily;[2] but Mr. Wood's inscriptions—many of them discovered in this very theatre—illustrated in particular some of the specific terms used in the chapter of the Acts. Thus they showed that the curious title 'Temple-keeper' or 'Sacristan' (lit. 'Temple-sweeper') 'of Artemis' (Acts xix. 35), was a title of honour used by the city;[3] and they also give examples of the use at Ephesus of the terms 'Asiarchs' (ver. 31), 'townclerk' or 'recorder' (ver. 35), 'proconsuls' (ver. 38), and 'regular [or stated] assembly' (ver. 39): the 'Asiarchs,' for instance, held a position of great dignity and influence; they were presidents of the confederation of the cities of Asia (τὸ κοινὸν τῆς Ἀσίας), and high-priests of the worship of the emperor, who presided also over certain festivals and games;[4] and the name of the 'recorder' at the time is specified at the end of nearly every decree.

In 1880 two inscriptions of Cyrus were published, one by Sir H. Rawlinson, the other by Mr. Pinches, which were found to throw

---

[1] *Corp. Inscr. Graec.*, No. 2954. See Bishop Lightfoot, *Contemp. Review*, May, 1878 (reprinted in *Essays on the work entitled Supernatural Religion*, 1889, p. 298); and comp. Headlam in *Authority and Archaeology*, p. 355 f.

[2] Comp., for instance, 'Not only in this city but everywhere temples are dedicated to the goddess, and statues erected and altars consecrated to her, on account of the manifest epiphanies which she vouchsafes,' with Acts xix. 27 'But also that the temple of the great goddess Artemis be made of no account, and that she should even be deposed from her magnificence, whom all Asia and the world worshippeth.'

[3] 'The city of the Ephesians . . . doubly [i. e. at two temples] *sacristan* of the Augusti, according to the decrees of the senate, and *sacristan of Artemis*, and friend of Augustus, entirely repaired and made good the awning of the theatre, after it had been torn, both from other sources and from what [was provided by] Tineius Sacerdos, the Proconsul' (Wood, Appendix, *Inscriptions from the Great Theatre*, No. 6, p. 51, from an inscription dating shortly after A.D. 219, the year in which Q. Tineius Sacerdos was consul); cf. Ramsay, in Hastings's *Dict. of the Bible*, i. 722 b.

[4] Wood, ibid., ii. 13 (p. 15), 'in accordance with a decree of T. Flavius Aristobulus, *Asiarch* and *recorder* of the people'; vi. 3 (p. 47) 'Publius Vedius Antoninus, the *Asiarch*, being *recorder*'; vi. 18 (p. 69), 'Tiberius Julius Rheginus, for the second time *Asiarch* of the temples in Ephesus, being perpetual president of the games'; cf. vi. 13 (p. 63), 'Tiberius Julius Rheginus, for the second time *high-priest* of the temples in Ephesus, being perpetual president of the games.'

important new light upon the reign of Nabo-na'id, the last native king of Babylon, the rise of Cyrus, and the circumstances under which he gained possession of Babylon. As early as 1854 Sir H. (then Major) Rawlinson had read the name of Belshazzar upon an Assyrian cylinder, found at Muqayyar (Ur)—a little south of the Euphrates, 130 miles south-east of Babylon; and it was known that he was the son, not of Nebuchadnezzar, as stated in the Book of Daniel, but of Nabo-na'id.[1] The two new inscriptions revolutionized many other old ideas about Cyrus and the events of his time. They showed, for instance, that Cyrus was not of Persian origin: he and his ancestors were kings of Anshan, a district of Elam; he only became 'king of Persia' afterwards. There was no siege of Babylon by Cyrus; his general, Gubaru, and afterwards he himself, both entered it without striking a blow: the account in Herodotus (i. 191) of the waters of the Euphrates having been diverted by Cyrus, and his troops then entering it while the inhabitants were feasting, is a romance; and the expressions in the Hebrew prophets, which were supposed to fall in with that account, are merely the poetic imagery in which the general thought of the impending doom of Babylon was clothed by them. Belshazzar also was never king of Babylon: he is called 'the king's son' to the day of his death; his father Nabo-na'id was king till Cyrus entered Babylon. Nor is there any room for 'Darius the Mede',[2] as king of Babylon; the contract-tablets pass from Nabo-na'id to Cyrus without a break. The Second Isaiah speaks of Bel and Nebo as doomed to go into exile, when Cyrus should take Babylon (Isa. xlvi. 1, 2), and the author of Jeremiah l. 2 declares that Bel and Merodach should be 'put to shame'; but Cyrus, in the proclamation contained in the other inscription, issued to the Babylonians shortly after his entry into the city, expresses his intention of honouring the gods of Babylon, attributes his successes to the guidance of Marduk, and hopes that prayers for his welfare may be offered before both Marduk, Bel, and Nebo. The prophets foresaw truly the fall of Babylon before Cyrus; but this inscription of Cyrus is one of many warnings that we have not to interpret the details of a prophet's predictions too literally.

In the same year (1880) Mr. Pinches published, from a small clay

---

[1] *Athenaeum*, March 18, 1854, p. 341 (in a letter from Baghdād). 'In the heart of Belshar-uzur, my firstborn, the offspring of my body, implant the fear of thy great divinity; may he not incline to sin; may he be filled with the fulness of life,' are the words of Nabo-na'id's prayer for his son (*Keilinschriftliche Bibliothek*, iii. 2, p. 97; similarly pp. 83, 85, 89).

[2] Dan. v. 31, vi. 1, 28, ix. 1.

tablet brought from the site of Babylon by the overseer of Mr. Rassam, a list of twenty-two kings, together with the lengths of their reigns, belonging to the first two dynasties of Babylon. From letters and contract-tablets, and from a contemporary chronicle, published by Mr. King from the collections in the British Museum, many more particulars of the reigns of these kings were afterwards learnt; but it was still generally supposed that the second dynasty of Mr. Pinches's tablet followed the first. A chronicle, published by Mr. King in 1907, proved, however, conclusively that Iluma-ilu, the first king of the second dynasty, was a contemporary of Shamshu-iluna and Abêshu, the seventh and eighth kings of the first dynasty, and the successors of Ḫammurabi. The newly discovered synchronism is important, as necessitating for Ḫammurabi a lower date, by at least a century, than that which had previously been assigned to him: it also affords an example of first conclusions being corrected by subsequent discoveries.

I must here turn aside for a moment from Babylonia to Egypt to mention that in 1883 M. Naville, by means of inscriptions discovered through excavation, fixed the site of Pithom, the store-city built by the Israelites in Egypt (Exod. i. 11), and determined the king, Rameses II (c. 1300–1234 B.C.), under whom it was built, and that in 1885 the same skilful explorer found the name, and ascertained the site, north-east of Cairo, of the biblical Goshen.

On the very important Tell el-Amarna letters, discovered in 1887, and the light thrown by them on Canaan in the fifteenth century B.C., I shall say something in my next lecture.

I must, however, mention now an important and interesting discovery made in 1901. Ḫammurabi—probably the Amraphel of Gen. xiv. 1—the sixth king of the first known dynasty of Babylon, who ruled for forty-three years at about 2150 B.C., was already known to us from an almost contemporary chronicle, and from numerous letters of his own and contract-tablets dating from his reign: we knew from these sources that he was an enterprising and successful ruler, who took an active personal interest in the welfare of his country, freed it from its foes, organized and consolidated its administration, and laid generally the foundation of its future greatness. But at the end of 1901, M. de Morgan, excavating at Susa, discovered a large block of black diorite, with a bas-relief representing Ḫammurabi receiving a code of laws from Shamash, the sun-god, and with the code of laws inscribed upon its front and back sides. About one-eighth of the code has been erased: the rest includes 248 separate enactments, on a great variety

HAMMURABI, KING OF BABYLON, RECEIVING HIS LAWS FROM THE SUN-GOD

From the upper part of the stelè (7½ feet high) on which his code of laws is inscribed. The Sun-god is represented as seated on a throne in the form of a temple façade, and his feet are resting upon the mountains. Photograph by Messrs. Mansell & Co.

From King and Hall's *Egypt and Western Asia in the Light of Recent Discoveries*, 1907, p. 265.

of subjects—laws relating to property, the duties and privileges of royal servants and other officials, the tenure, rent, and cultivation of land, trade and commerce, family law (including, for instance, the rights of wife and children, divorce, inheritance, adoption), criminal law (penalties for different kinds of assault), laws fixing the rates of payment for the hire of different articles, and the rates of wages in different employments, and laws relating to slavery. It will be seen at once what a variety of subjects the code embraces, and what an advanced stage of civilization, with commerce, agriculture, and other branches of industry fully developed, it presupposes on the part of the people whose life it was designed to regulate. Naturally, the laws were not all new: Hammurabi reduced to a code—doubtless, in particular cases, introducing additions and modifications of his own— a system of law and custom which had been for long in operation in the country. A deal has been written on this code: it is the most ancient code of laws known to us; and its relation to other ancient systems of law, and the extent of its influence, have both been much debated. Its provisions are never of a ritual or ceremonial character: they relate mostly to what we call civil and criminal law; and a considerable number of them are remarkably similar to corresponding provisions of the Hebrew codes preserved in the Pentateuch. It is impossible to give examples here:[1] Hammurabi's code embraces a large number of subjects which do not enter into Hebrew law at all; still, in the parts which cover the same ground, there are resemblances which call for explanation. Probably the most satisfactory explanation will be found to be that, while *direct* borrowing on the part of the Hebrew legislators is not probable, the two codes do stand in some *indirect* relation towards each other: either both, in the provisions which are similar, exhibit independent codifications of old, customary Semitic usage, common to the ancestors of both the Babylonians and the Hebrews; or some knowledge of Hammurabi's laws reached the Hebrews indirectly—perhaps through the Canaanites, who, as we shall see in the next lecture, were for some centuries profoundly influenced by Babylonia—and determined the form and character of some of the provisions of Hebrew law. But our present knowledge does not enable us to do more than put forward conjectures on the subject, any one of which may be shown by future discoveries to be incorrect.

I close with a few words on the most recent archaeological dis-

---

[1] See Stanley A. Cook, *The Laws of Moses and the Code of Hammurabi* (1903); and Johns in Hastings's *Dict. of the Bible*, v. 584-612 (including a translation of the entire code).

coveries of all, which come to us from Egypt. In the spring of 1904 Mr. (now Dr.) Robert Mond, a patron of science and learning alike, while excavating at Thebes in Upper Egypt, heard that some Hebrew papyri had been found near Assuan, the ancient garrison town of Syene. His interest was awakened; and he at once took measures to secure them. Upon examination they were found to be not Hebrew, but Aramaic. The papyri themselves were presented by Mr. Mond to the Cairo Museum; but photographic facsimiles were sent to England; and these, together with certain other papyri found at the same place, ten in all, were edited by Prof. Sayce and Dr. Cowley in 1906, in an exceptionally complete and sumptuous form, due to the munificence of Dr. Mond. The entire collection proved to be one of great interest. It consisted of legal documents, belonging mostly to successive generations of a Jewish family settled at Elephantine—another garrison town on an island opposite to Syene—and dated from the fifteenth year of Xerxes (471 B.C.) to the thirteenth of Darius II (411 B.C.). One Mahseiah, son of Yedoniah, owns land in Elephantine, which he holds by a deed of conveyance from its former owner, Dargman. On the marriage of his daughter, Mibtahiah, to a neighbour, Jezaniah, in 459, he assigns her this land as her marriage-portion, to herself and her heirs for ever, at the same time giving to her husband Dargman's deed of conveyance. Thirteen years afterwards, in 446, Mahseiah makes over to his daughter some house-property which he had bought from Meshullam, together with the deed of sale. Shortly after this Mibtahiah is married to a second husband, Ashor; and one of the papyri (G) is a marriage-contract enumerating the articles which Ashor gave as the *mohar*, or marriage-price, of Mibtahiah. By 421 the sons of this marriage, Yedoniah and Mahseiah—they bear the same names as their great-grandfather and grandfather—are grown up, and have to sustain an action brought by their cousins, the nephews of their mother's first husband, to recover the house which their mother, in accordance with the testamentary powers given her by her father, had bequeathed to her sons by her second marriage. Lastly, there is a deed by which Mahseiah and Yedoniah agree to divide their mother's slaves between them. We are struck by the legal precision with which deeds relating to all these transactions are drawn up—the exact description, for instance, of the situation of the property mentioned, the precise phraseology in which a claim is renounced or a right conferred, the care with which provision is made for the rebutment of future claims, and the manner in which each deed is attested by a number of witnesses. But similar precision in the framing of conveyances, contracts, and other legal deeds is usual in the ancient world, and is found in Babylonian deeds even of the Hammurabi period. The technical terms used in these papyri are in some cases those of Babylonian law, which no doubt reached Egypt through the Persians. Elephantine is some 400 miles south of Cairo, just north of the first cataract; and it is surprising—though, it is true, we knew that there were Jews in Egypt in Jeremiah's time[1]—to find a colony of Jews settled there. These papyri give us some insight into the conditions under which they lived. It is also surprising to find a notice of a 'temple of the god Yahu' (i. e. Yahweh, Jehovah)— the word for 'temple' is not Hebrew or Aramaic, but Babylonian— though it is only referred to incidentally as adjoining two of the houses mentioned (E 14, J 6), and so fixing their situation. Maḥseiah also swears by the god Yahu in establishing his right to the house claimed by Dargman (B 4, 6, 11). Mibtaḥiah, however, swears by Sati, the Egyptian goddess of the cataracts (F 5).

Within less than a year of the publication of these papyri, in 1907, Elephantine furnished a still greater surprise. A German explorer, Dr. Rubensohn, excavating in the mound which marks the site of the ancient Elephantine, found a number of other Aramaic papyri, which were sent to Berlin, and examined by Dr. Sachau, Professor of Semitic Languages, and Director of the Oriental Seminary, at Berlin, and also, I may add, Corresponding Member of this Academy. The whole collection has not yet been published; but three, of special interest, were published by Dr. Sachau last autumn. The first of these—dating from 408 B.C., only three years after the last of the Assuan papyri—is a petition from the Jewish colony at Elephantine to Bagohi—the Bagoas of Josephus—the Persian governor of Judah, to crave his intervention and help. During the temporary absence of the Persian governor of Egypt, the priests of the ram-headed Egyptian god Chnub had bribed Waidrang, the commander of the garrison in Elephantine, to destroy the temple of the god Yahu, of which we have already heard; and they entreat Bagohi, and also Delaiah and Shelemiah, the sons of Sanballat, the governor of Samaria, to use their influence to obtain permission for them to rebuild it. And in their petition they give very interesting particulars about the temple. It had been built for more than 120 years; and it had been respected by Cambyses when he conquered Egypt, and

---

[1] Jer. xliv. 1, 15, 24.

made it a Persian province, in 525 B.C. It was a substantial and handsome building, with pillars of stone, and seven stone gates. It was used, not like a synagogue, for prayer only, but also for sacrifice; it had an altar, upon which burnt-offerings, meal-offerings, and frankincense were regularly offered; and the gold and silver bowls, used for tossing the sacrificial blood against the sides of the altar, bear the same name as those used in the Temple of Jerusalem. The petitioners deplore the ruin of their sanctuary and the cessation of worship in it; they say that since it happened they have put on sackcloth, and fasted, and prayed, and not anointed themselves with oil or drunk wine; and they promise that, if Bagohi can obtain for them what they ask, they will, when the Temple is rebuilt, ever remember him in their prayers and offer sacrifices in his name. The second papyrus is only a mutilated duplicate of the first; the third is a short memorandum of the reply sent by Bagohi and Delaiah, to the effect that the petition had been granted, and the Temple could be rebuilt. These papyri bring us very near to the Old Testament. They were written only fifty years after Ezra brought back a second company of exiles from Babylon to Judah, and only twenty-four years after Nehemiah's second visit to Jerusalem, in 432. We breathe in them an atmosphere very similar to that into which we are brought by the Aramaic letters and edicts in the Book of Ezra; and many of the words and expressions are the same, or similar. The point, however, which particularly surprises us is the existence of a Temple, with an altar, and with sacrifices offered upon it, outside Jerusalem. Whatever the cause may be, the Jews of Elephantine did not feel themselves bound by the law of the single sanctuary, so strongly insisted on by the writer of Deuteronomy, and accepted as an unquestioned principle in the priestly sections of the Pentateuch. It is well within the limits of possibility that, thanks to the dry Egyptian climate, other documents of not less interest may be discovered in the same place; and all must heartily wish that this may be the case.

Though they do not bear directly upon biblical science, I may at least, before I finish, allude briefly to the extensive excavations which have been carried on by German explorers in the huge mound of Kal'at Sherkāt, which marks the site of the ancient 'city of Asshur', on the right bank of the Tigris, some fifty miles south of Nineveh, repeatedly mentioned by the Assyrian kings, and the capital of Assyria long before Nineveh acquired that pre-eminence. Inscriptions have been found there, throwing light upon early periods of Assyrian history, previously little known. Nor must I close without at least alluding to

HITTITE INSCRIPTIONS FROM BOGHAZ-KEUI

the excavations carried on in 1906 and 1907 by Prof. Winckler at Boghaz-keui, the old capital of the Hittites, in the modern province of Angora, the ancient Cappadocia. Here, in what seem to have been the archives of the ancient Hittite kings, a very extensive collection of cuneiform inscriptions, expressing partly the language of Babylonia, partly the native language of the country, has been discovered, not only giving much information about the history and political condition of the Hittites and neighbouring peoples, but also testifying to the brisk political correspondence carried on at this distant time between the Hittite kings and other nations, including even Egypt, in the language of Babylonia. It is striking evidence of the wide-reaching influence of Babylonia in the ancient world, to find Cappadocia and Egypt corresponding in its language and script. These inscriptions have not as yet been published; but a fairly full account of them has been given by Prof. Winckler.[1] New discoveries may be looked for from this quarter; and it may be hoped, among other things, as some of the inscriptions are bilingual, being written in both Hittite and Babylonian, that the decipherment of the Hittite inscriptions may be advanced by their means.

In my next two lectures I shall endeavour to give some account of what we have learnt more particularly about Palestine, partly from inscriptions, partly from excavation.

[1] *Mitteilungen der Deutschen Orient-Gesellschaft*, No. 35 (Berlin, Dec. 1907). Cf. King and Hall, op. cit. (above, p. 7), pp. 468 ff.

Note on p. 10.

The works referred to are—A. P. Stanley's *Sinai and Palestine in connexion with their history*, 1856 (new edition, 1866); and G. A. Smith's *Historical Geography of the Holy Land*, 1894 (ed. 4, with additions, 1897); to which may be added now the last-named writer's two fine volumes, *Jerusalem. The Topography, Economics, and History from the earliest times to A. D. 70* (1907).

II. CANAAN, AS KNOWN THROUGH INSCRIPTIONS AND EXCAVATION

ON the condition of Canaan before the Hebrew occupation new and surprising light has recently been thrown by the discoveries now commonly associated with the name of Tell el-Amarna. Tell el-Amarna is a spot about 170 miles south of Cairo, the site of a new capital built by Amenhotep IV of the XVIIIth Dynasty, as a centre for the worship of the sun-god, whom he revered as the source of all life, power, and force in the universe.[1] Some *fellaḥin*, digging here in 1887, came upon a chamber containing several hundred clay tablets, inscribed with the familiar cuneiform characters of Babylonia. At first, strange to say, these were regarded, even by authorities who ought to have known better, as deserving no attention: a number were carried in sacks to Luxor to be hawked about among the dealers there, and these were largely broken or spoilt on the way. Those that escaped this fate, numbering altogether about 290, and filling in a translation about 200 octavo pages, were in the end bought up for either museums (81 are in the British Museum, Table-Case F) or private collections; and proved, upon examination, to be a part of the official archives of Amenhotep III (1414–1383 B.C.) and Amenhotep IV (1383–1365 B.C.), and to consist chiefly of letters and reports addressed to these kings by their officials, and by foreign potentates having relations with Egypt. The latter, about forty in number, are principally from kings of Alashia (Cyprus), the Hittites (on the north of Palestine), the Mitanni (in the north-west of the later Mesopotamia, between, speaking roughly, Aleppo and Nineveh), Babylonia, and Assyria. These are letters in which the writers generally express their desire to maintain friendly relations with the Egyptian kings, or send them complimentary greetings: in one, for instance, the king of Alashia protests that he has no alliance with the Lukki (i.e. Syrian pirates), who, on the contrary,

---

[1] See Petrie, *History of Egypt*, ii. 211 ff., with the striking hymn to Aten, celebrating him as the source of life in men and animals, as watering the earth, causing the seasons, &c., pp. 215–18 (also in Breasted, *History of Egypt*, 1906, pp. 371 ff.). The title Khu-n-Aten (or Ikhn-aton), assumed by him, is often supposed to mean 'Glory of the Solar Disk', and to be an expression of his devotion to the sun-god: but this, Mr. F. Ll. Griffith tells me, is uncertain.

yearly plunder Alashia; if Alashians are proved to have plundered, they shall be punished.[1] These letters are of interest as showing the extent and character of diplomatic communication at the time; we can now supplement them, as was mentioned in Lecture I (p. 31), by the correspondence which preceded the treaty concluded a little later (p. 38) between the Hittites of Cappadocia and Egypt. The maintenance of facilities for commercial intercourse between the different countries was also evidently regarded as important.[2] The other letters, which constitute the bulk of the correspondence, are principally from governors stationed by the Egyptian kings at various places in Palestine, Phoenicia, and Syria. It had, indeed, been long known that the Pharaohs of this age, especially Thothmes I and III, shortly before Amenhotep III, and Seti I and Rameses II, of the following dynasty, had led their victorious armies over Western Asia. Thothmes III, for instance, gives in his annals a graphic description of his expedition in his twenty-third year (1480 B.C.)—his departure from Egypt, his arrival before Megiddo, in the plain of Esdraelon, the battle and siege of the fortress, its capitulation, with a picture of its prostrate chiefs 'smelling the ground' at his feet, the abundance of gold and silver and other valuables which he took from it, and the successes won by him afterwards further north and east, in Phoenicia, Syria, and Upper Mesopotamia, and the tribute exacted by him from these countries.[3] If Thothmes' statements are to be trusted, the Canaanites of Megiddo must have been wealthy, and have lived in luxury, at the time; for they are mentioned as having chariots of silver and gold; and many gold and silver articles, inlaid tables, and other valuables are stated to have been taken by the Egyptians as spoil.[4] And engraved on the walls of his temple at Karnak, he has left a list of 350 places conquered by him in these countries, of which 119 are within, or near, the borders of Canaan.[5] It was not, however, known what means the Egyptians adopted to organize and maintain the power which they thus acquired. The Tell el-Amarna correspondence shows that, at about 1400 B.C., Palestine and the neighbouring countries formed an Egyptian province, under the rule of Egyptian governors stationed in the principal towns, and, what is more remarkable, communicating with the Egyptian king in the Babylonian language. This last-named circumstance is particularly noticeable. It is not that a Babylonian

---

[1] Petrie, *Egypt and Syria from the Tell el-Amarna Letters* (1898), p. 46.
[2] Letters 6, 11, 256.
[3] Petrie, *Hist. of Egypt*, ii. 103-23; cf. 126 (the *stelè* on the Euphrates).
[4] Ibid. pp. 107, 108, 110-12.   [5] Ibid. pp. 320-32.

king himself uses the Babylonian language: kings of Cyprus and the Mitanni and Egyptian governors in Palestine do the same; and even letters written in Palestine and addressed to others than the Egyptian king are in Babylonian likewise. This standing use of Babylonian can be explained only in one way, by the fact viz. that for long previously Canaan and the neighbouring countries had been under Babylonian influence. When, or how, this influence began we do not definitely know: we are hardly in a position to affirm that it had been continuous since the days when Sargon (*c.* 3800 [or ? 2800] B.C.), Ḥammurabi (*c.* 2150 B.C.[1]), and Ammiditana (*c.* 2050) claimed authority over the 'West' land; but, at all events, Canaan had remained under it so long that, at least for official purposes, the practice of using the language and writing of Babylonia continued to prevail, even after Canaan had become a province of the Egyptian empire. The fact is important. Primarily, no doubt, the influence was political; but it would naturally bring with it elements of civilization, of arts and sciences, of mythology and religious belief. Even among the Tell el-Amarna tablets there have been found fragments of Babylonian mythological tales. It *may* thus have been through the Canaanites that the Babylonian traditions and beliefs—or, at least, in some cases, the echoes of them—which we find in the early chapters of Genesis reached the Hebrews.

It would occupy too much time, and also be unnecessary for our present purpose, to describe the contents of these letters in detail. They have been analysed in full by Professor Petrie in his volume *Syria and Egypt from the Tell el-Amarna Letters* (1898). We learn from them in general that the Egyptians were losing their hold upon Syria: they either did not care, or were not able, to spare the troops necessary to keep it in hand; their power was threatened partly by the Hittites and other powerful neighbours, especially a certain people called in the letters of Abdi-ḥiba *Ḥabiri*,[2] partly by the native population, partly by intrigues and rivalries between the Egyptian governors themselves. Accordingly the writers of the reports frequently dilate upon the dangers to which they are exposed, beg earnestly for assistance, bring charges of disloyalty against other governors, and protest emphatically their own fidelity. The principal districts and places men-

---

[1] Thureau-Dangin's date is B.C. 2130–2088, Poebel's 2198–2155 (*Z. f. Assyr.* 1908, pp. 186, 175).

[2] In the other letters, the people which play the same part are called by an ideogram, which, read phonetically, would be pronounced SA-GAS. See, on the question involved, Winckler, *Die Keilinschriften u. das A. T.*, ed. 3 (1902), p. 196 f.; Knudtzon (below, p. 35, note 2), p. 51 f. There *may* be some connexion between the 'Ḥabiri' and the 'Hebrews': the two cannot be identical, but the Hebrews may, for instance, have been a branch of them.

tioned are, in the far north, the land of the Amurru (the Amorites), Zurru (Tyre), Ziduna (Zidon), Birutu (Beirut), Gubla (Gebal, Byblus), Zumur (Simyra, now *Sumra*, about seventy miles north of Beirut: Heb. Zĕmar, Gen. x. 18); in the north of Palestine, Akka (Acco), and Magidda (Megiddo); in the south, Joppa, Gezer, Urusalim (Jerusalem), Ashkelon, Lachish, and Gaza: all these are under Egyptian governors. In the end all seem to have deserted Egypt: some voluntarily, others because no efficient help was forthcoming, and circumstances were too strong for them to hold out longer. In the north the leaders of revolt were—in spite of his protestations of being the king's most faithful servant—Abdashirta, governor of the Amorites, and his sons, especially the energetic Aziru. Ribaddi, governor of Phoenicia (from whom we have sixty-two letters), was faithful to Egypt; and betakes himself from one Phoenician city to another, from Gebal to Zemar, then to Gebal and Beirut, and to Gebal and Beirut again, till finally he is left with Gebal alone, with the enemy at the gate,[1] after which we lose sight of him. Six of the letters[2] are from Abdi-ḥiba, the governor of Urusalim. Till the time of David, we may remark in passing, a tribe called Jebusites still held Jerusalem; and from Judges xix. 10, 11 and 1 Chron. xi. 4, 5 it used commonly to be supposed that till then Jebus had been the name of Jerusalem; but these letters now show that this was not the case: the name of the city was Jerusalem from the first, and the old name Jebus was falsely inferred from the name of the tribe which in the early centuries of the Hebrew occupation dwelt in it. Abdi-ḥiba also, like so many of the other governors, is in difficulties. He is hard pressed by the Ḥabiri; the neighbouring cities of Gezer, Lachish, and Ashkelon are aiding the enemy; he has been slandered to the king, and accused of disloyalty. But he protests emphatically his innocence: he owes his throne, like Addu-nirari, king of Nuḥassi, before him,[3] and like Jehoiakim long afterwards, not to any hereditary privilege, but to the favour of the Egyptian king:

To the king, my lord, my sun: Abdi-ḥiba, thy servant, at the feet of the king, my lord, seven and seven times I fall down. Behold, the king, my lord, has laid his name on the East and on the West. It is a calumny, what they

[1] Winckler, No. 67; Petrie, No. 225.
[2] In Winckler's edition (*Keilinschriftliche Bibliothek*, v, 1896), Nos. 179, 180, 181, 182ª + 185 + 182ᵇ [see Sayce, *Archaeology of the Cuneiform Inscriptions*, 1907, p. 202 f.], 183, 184; perhaps also 186 (the name is obliterated): in Knudzton's more recent edition (1908), Nos. 285–290.
[3] Whom Thothmes III, as a letter of his grandson in the Tell el-Amarna correspondence states, had installed and anointed (Winckler, No. 37 [where the name is read *Ramman-nirari*]; Knudzton, No. 51).

allege against me. Behold, I am no prince : I am an officer of the king, my lord, I am one who brings him tribute. Behold, neither my father nor my mother established me in this place : the arm of the mighty king has caused me to enter the house of my father.

Gratitude alone, therefore, would have preserved Abdi-ḥiba from the thought of plotting against one to whom he owed so much. He is beset by foes, and begs earnestly for troops: if they are not sent the country is lost to Egypt: 'The Ḥabiri are capturing the fortresses of the king. Not a single governor remains among them to the king, my lord: all have perished. May the king, my lord, send help to his country. If no troops come this year, all the countries of the king, my lord, will be utterly destroyed.' In the last letter that we have from him the same request is repeated. What happened to Abdi-ḥiba in the end we do not know; perhaps, like many of the other princes and chiefs when they saw that they were unsupported, he found himself obliged to join the Ḥabiri.

The picture thus given of Palestine between about 1414 and 1365 B.C.—probably some 200 years before the Hebrew invasion—as a province of Egypt, in which the ruling class made use of the language of Babylonia, is entirely new to us; it could not, from notices in the Old Testament, have been in the least suspected. One or two features in the picture remain, however, still to be noticed. I have already referred to the interesting particulars about Jerusalem, and the correction which Abdi-ḥiba's letters supply to the old supposition that the name of the city was originally Jebus. A word must, however, also be said on the position occupied by the Amorites. In the Hebrew traditions of the conquests of Canaan they are represented as occupying partly a region on the east of Jordan, north-east of the Dead Sea, ruled by Sihon, partly a considerable portion of the territory west of Jordan ; but in the Tell el-Amarna letters it is clear that they are limited to a particular area on the north of Palestine, behind Phoenicia—an area which the inscriptions discovered recently at Boghaz-keui seem to have shown extended eastwards across the great Syrian desert to the border of Babylonia.[1] They appear in the same locality in the inscriptions of Seti I and Rameses II of the XIXth Dynasty, and even in those of Rameses III of the XXth Dynasty, after the time of the Exodus. We must suppose that, while the district east of Phoenicia continued to retain the name of 'land of Amar', branches of the 'Amorites' advanced to the south, and obtained a footing on the territory both east and west of the Jordan, afterwards occupied by the Israelites.

[1] *Mitteilungen der Deutschen Orient-Gesellschaft*, No. 35 (Dec. 1907), p. 25 f.

THE TELL EL-AMARNA LETTERS

The other feature which must not be overlooked is the light which the letters throw upon the native population of Canaan. The letters, as has been stated, are written in Babylonian, a language which, though allied to Hebrew, as the paradigms and numerous words immediately show, is by no means identical with it: but from time to time Canaanite words appear in them, being used either independently or for the purpose of glossing or explaining a Babylonian expression in the more familiar dialect of the scribe who was writing the dispatch: and these Canaanite words are hardly distinguishable from Hebrew. The principal and clearest of these are enumerated by Zimmern in the third edition of the *Cuneiform Inscriptions and the O. T.*, p. 652 f. The letters thus show that the pre-Israelitish inhabitants of Canaan were closely akin to the Hebrews, and that they spoke substantially the same language. The same fact follows from many of the names of places preserved to us in the Egyptian inscriptions, and also from others, older to all appearance than the period of the Hebrew occupation, mentioned in the Old Testament, which are evidently explicable from roots current in Hebrew. Divided religiously, the Hebrews and the Canaanites were in language and civilization closely allied.

Expeditions through Canaan into Phoenicia and North Syria were made also by the kings of the XIXth Dynasty. On the north wall of the great hypostyle hall at Karnak built by Seti I (Petrie, 1326-1300 B.C.; Breasted, 1313-1292 B.C.) is a fine series of scenes illustrating various events in the Syrian campaign of his first year; and elsewhere on his monuments lists are given of the cities taken by him; but, though they extend as far north as Aleppo, they do not include many in Canaan itself.[1] A monument, if not of his campaign, at least of his rule over Syria, and perhaps of an Egyptian garrison stationed at the place, is still preserved in the form of a *stelè*, inscribed with his cartouche, discovered by G. A. Smith in May, 1900, at Tell esh-Shihāb, twenty-two miles east of the south end of the Sea of Tiberias, on the east of Jordan.[2] Seti's son, Rameses II (1300-1234 B.C.; or 1292-1225 B.C.)—if the Israelites, as Exod. i. 11 states, built Pithom and Raamses, the Pharaoh of the oppression—led expeditions into Syria in his second, fourth, fifth, and eighth years; in his fifth year he gained the famous victory over the Hittites at Kedesh on the Orontes, which was celebrated by the court poet Pentaur[3]: in his twenty-first year was concluded his treaty with the Hittites, the

---

[1] Petrie, *Hist. of Egypt*, iii. 11-16, 16-17.
[2] *Quarterly Statement of the Palestine Exploration Fund*, 1901, 347, 348; 1904, 78-80.   [3] Petrie, *Hist. of Egypt*, iii. 45-61.

earliest treaty at present known to history, and a most important document, acquainting us with the diplomatic usages current at the time, and also giving valuable information about the political relations subsisting between the two nations.[1] The Egyptian text of this treaty had been known for long: it was an archaeological surprise when in 1907 Prof. Winckler discovered at Boghaz-keui portions of the Babylonian version, together with a number of letters, all written in cuneiform, showing that considerable diplomatic correspondence had preceded the conclusion of the treaty.[2] And the monolith of basalt, called by tradition 'Job's Stone', at Sheikh Sa'd, eleven miles north-north-east of Tell esh-Shihāb, representing the Egyptian king worshipping before a non-Egyptian deity crowned with a large lunar crescent, is still a monument of the authority exercised by Rameses II over this part of Syria.[3] There exists, moreover, a curious and interesting papyrus, called *The Travels of a Mohar*, written during the same reign, the author of which, as it seems, rallies an acquaintance with his boasted exploits and adventures, and depicts him as a Mohar, or Assyrian military commander, visiting various places in Canaan.[4] Among the places mentioned by him are Gebal, Beirut, Zidon, Zarephath, and Tyre, in Phoenicia; Achshaph (Josh. xi. 1); the 'mountain of User'—a name which has been supposed to indicate that the tribe of Asher was already in pre-Mosaic times settled in the north of Canaan; the 'mountain of Sakama' (Shechem); Hazor (Josh. xi. 1); Kiriath-Anab and Beth-sopher—probably scribal errors for *Beth*-anab (Anab in the hill-country of Judah, Josh. xv. 50), and *Kiriath*-sopher (the Kiriath-sepher of Josh. xv. 15); Beth-sha-el, the *Babylonian* equivalent of Bethel, shewing that the writer had somehow obtained the name through a cuneiform channel; Megiddo, Joppa, and Gaza. This document combines with other indications to show that since Thothmes III had made Syria an Egyptian province, Palestine was known in Egypt, and that there was a good deal of intercourse between the two countries.

Rameses II's successor, Merenptah (1234–1214 or 1225–1215), was in all probability the Pharaoh of the Exodus. An inscription of his, found by Professor Petrie in 1896 in the king's funeral temple at Thebes, contains the earliest mention of 'Israel' known at present to

---

[1] Ibid. pp. 63–8.
[2] *Mitteilungen der Deutschen Orient-Gesellschaft*, No. 35, p. 20 f.
[3] Hastings's *Dict. of the Bible*, i. 166ᵇ; or, more fully, Schumacher in the *Ztschr. des Deutschen Palästina-Vereins*, 1892, pp. 142 ff., and Erman, *ibid.* 1893, pp. 205 ff.
[4] See Erman, *Life in Ancient Egypt*, pp. 380 ff.; Sayce, *Patriarchal Palestine*, p. 204 f., 209–24; W. Max Müller, *Asien und Europa nach altägyptischen Denkmälern*, pp. 57, 184–7, 394.

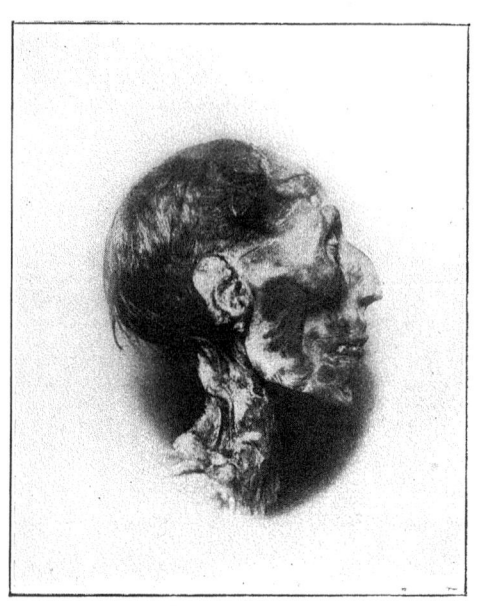

HEAD OF MUMMY OF RAMESES II
Discovered by Prof. Maspero in 1881 at Deir el-Baḥari, opposite to Karnak (Thebes), and now in the Gizeh Museum.
From a photograph.

GRANITE BUST OF MERENPTAH
From Merenptah's Temple at Thebes.
From Petrie's *History of Egypt*, iii (1905), 108.

[*To face p.* 39]

occur on any monument. It had for long been known that Merenptah in his fifth year had gained at Prosopis a great victory over the Libyans, who had invaded the Delta with a large body of allies: the narrative of his success, inscribed at Karnak, may be read at length in Brugsch's *History of Egypt* (the one-vol. ed.), pp. 311 ff., or, somewhat abridged, in Maspero's *Struggle of the Nations*, pp. 431 ff.[1] The inscription found by Professor Petrie consists, for the greater part, of a grandiloquent description of the same occurrence: no more, says the author, is the land disturbed with preparations for repelling the invader, Egypt is again at peace:—

No longer is there the lament of sighing man. The villages are again settled. He who has tilled his crop will eat it. Ra has turned himself (favourably) to Egypt. King Merenptah is born for the purpose of avenging it. Chiefs are prostrate, saying, ' Salām ' (i. e. supplicating for mercy). Not one among the Nine Bows (the barbarians) raises his head. Vanquished are the Tehenna (Libyans); the Khita (Hittites) are pacified. Canaan is seized with every evil; Ashkelon is carried away; Gezer is taken; Yenoam is annihilated; *Ysiraal is desolated, its seed* (or *fruit*) *is not*. Charu (perhaps the Horites, the old population of Edom) has become as widows for Egypt (i. e. is helpless before the attacks of Egypt); all lands together are at peace. Every one that was a marauder hath been subdued by King Merenptah, who gives life like the sun every day.

This is the earliest mention of Israel in any inscription at present known: the next known to us is nearly four centuries later, when Shalmaneser II mentions Ahab, king of Israel, at the battle of Karkar in 854. The terms in which Merenptah speaks of Israel are surprising. The people is so mentioned by the side of conquered peoples or places in Canaan as to imply, almost necessarily, that it was also in Canaan itself. It is difficult to avoid the inference that, though the Bible represents Jacob and all his sons going down into Egypt, and makes no mention of any of his descendents returning to Palestine till after the Exodus, some Israelites must either have remained all the time in Palestine, or have returned thither, perhaps after the end of the famine.[2] As we have seen, a place in Palestine that may contain the name of the tribe Asher is mentioned in the time of Rameses II; and still earlier, in Thothmes III's lists of conquests, there are two names (Nos. 78 and 102) which, transliterated into Hebrew, would become Joseph-el and Jacob-el. The coincidences with the names of two of the patriarchs is remarkable: still, it may be accidental; Joseph and Jacob, in the names quoted, may be simply two verbal forms. The Biblical accounts of the Exodus

---

[1] Cf. the summary in Petrie, *History of Egypt*, iii. 108-13.
[2] Cf. Petrie, ibid. p. 114.

40 CANAAN AS KNOWN THROUGH EXCAVATION

are not contemporary: the writers to whom we owe them concentrate their attention upon the Israelites who made their escape from Egypt, and may not have known anything of their brethren already in Palestine. The inscription raises more questions than it solves. We must hold our judgement in suspense, and hope that some further discovery may clear up the problems which it sets before us.

I may now proceed to speak of excavation in Palestine. The accompanying map will show the situation of the places recently excavated

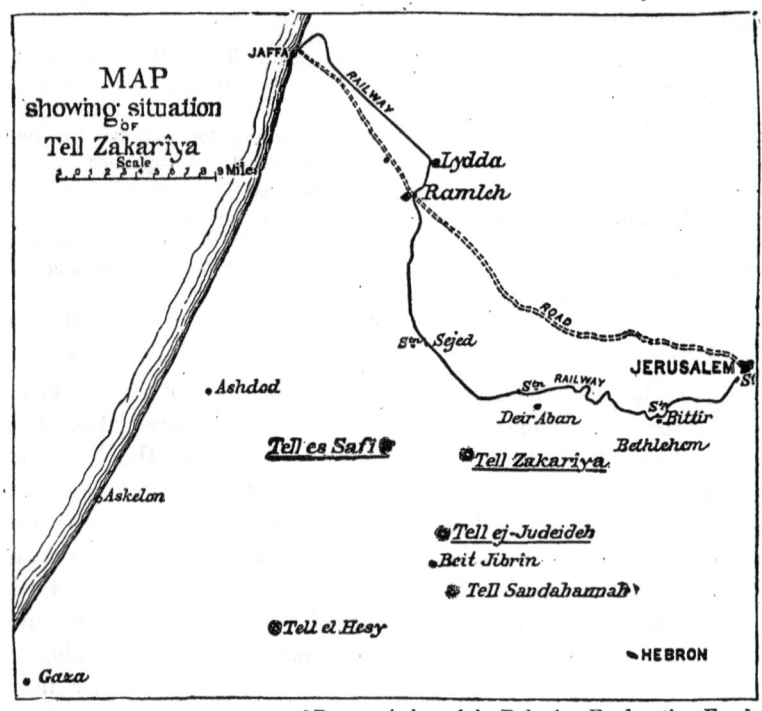

[*By permission of the Palestine Exploration Fund.*]

MAP OF SOUTH-WEST JUDAH, SHOWING THE SITES EXCAVATED
From Bliss and Macalister's *Excavations in Palestine*, p. 2.

in the south of Palestine, viz. (1) Tell el-Ḥesy, a fortress at the foot of the valley leading up to Hebron, and looking out over the Philistine plain towards Ashkelon; (2) Gezer, on a projecting ridge looking out towards Joppa, on which I shall say more later; (3) four places, excavated by Dr. Bliss and Mr. Macalister in 1898–1900 with many valuable results, though I shall not have much occasion to refer to them for my present purpose, viz. Tell eṣ-Ṣāfi, the 'Mound of the Shining Cliff', the Blanche Garde of the Crusaders, so called from the

[*By permission of the Palestine Exploration Fund.*

The Mound of Tell el-Ḥesy, from the North-east, showing the part excavated

From F. J. Bliss, *A Mound of Many Cities.* Frontispiece.

white cliffs, 300 feet high, on which it stands, at the foot of the vale of Elah leading up to Jerusalem, and looking down across the plain towards Ashdod, Tell Zakariya (so called from a chapel of Zechariah, the father of John the Baptist), Tell ej-Judeideh, and Tell Sandahannah (the 'Mound of St. Anna'). In addition to these places there are (4) Taanach and (5) Megiddo, in the north of Palestine, excavated by Professor Sellin and Dr. Schumacher respectively (above, p. 10), the discoveries made at which, as they often illustrate those made at Gezer, I shall refer to from time to time.

I will begin with Tell el-Ḥesy, where Professor Petrie, during the six weeks spent by him there in 1890, laid the foundations of scientific excavation in Palestine. The work thus auspiciously begun by Professor Petrie in 1890 was continued by Dr. Bliss, and ended—I cannot say completed, for two-thirds of the Tell had to be left unexplored[1]—in Jan. 1893. Tell el-Ḥesy is a large hill thirty-three miles south-west of Jerusalem, and fourteen miles from the sea-coast, on the south bank of the torrent-stream called the Wādy el-Ḥesy. The Arabic 'Tell' is the same word as the Heb. *tēl*, a 'mound', used both of the mound which might conceal the remains of a ruined city, and of a mound of the same kind on which in after times another inhabited city might itself stand. Thus Ai was made a 'desolate *mound*', Josh. viii. 28 (cf. Deut. xiii. 16, Jer. xlix. 2); and Jeremiah, in a promise of restoration, says, 'The city shall be builded *on its own mound*' (Jer. xxx. 18; cf. Josh. xi. 13). There are many such mounds in Palestine: they may rise to a considerable height above the surrounding plain, and may cover an extensive area. A 'tell' is in appearance an ordinary hill; but it is in reality, at least in its upper part, a mass of ruins. In the East, from the earliest times, buildings have been constructed of sun-dried bricks, blocks of mud held together by chopped straw. A city was built of houses made in this way; and after a while, either from war or from decay, the mud houses fell to pieces; streets and rooms were filled with remains of the fallen walls; the level of the streets also was often raised independently by the accumulation of refuse in them; and when, as often happened, the city was rebuilt on its former site, it naturally stood some feet above the original city. This process might naturally be repeated; and the excavation of Tell el-Ḥesy showed that it had actually been repeated there ten times, so that the Tell was veritably, as Dr. Bliss called his book that describes it, a 'Mound of many cities'. The natural hill on which the first of these cities had been built rose to fifty or sixty feet above the neighbouring stream: but above this there were some

[1] Bliss, *A Mound of Many Cities*, p. 59.

sixty feet of débris, consisting of a succession of distinct strata, each four or five feet thick, and each distinguished from the adjoining strata by the distinctive character of its remains. By the distinctness and regularity of the strata composing it, Tell el-Ḥesy proved in fact an ideal place for the excavator. It especially showed clearly the characteristics of the pottery peculiar to different periods of the history—Canaanite, Phoenician, Jewish, and Greek; and thus provided a key to the archaeology of Palestine, which has proved very valuable to subsequent explorers.

In giving some description of these successive strata, it will be convenient to begin with the earliest or lowest, though of course that was actually uncovered the last. In the process of excavation, as each stratum was laid bare, disclosing, for instance, as was often the case, a number of small rectangular compartments, separated from one another by low walls—the remains of ancient houses and other buildings—it was measured, planned, and photographed, and the various objects found in it were carefully tabulated. The first settlement spread over an area of nearly a quarter of a mile square. Remains of a great tower 56 by 28 feet, with walls 9 to 10 feet thick, enclosing chambers about 10 feet square, as well as of other rooms and walls, were found in it, together with various bronze implements, and also pottery of a type called 'Amorite', or, better—for, if the Tell el-Amarna letters are to be trusted, there were no Amorites in Canaan at this early date—pre-Israelite or Canaanite, which, by its shape and facings, is clearly distinguishable both from Phoenician on the one hand, and from Egyptian on the other.[1] In some parts there were ruins of houses one above the other; hence the remains in this stratum as a whole are termed by Dr. Bliss City sub I and City I. For reasons which will appear immediately their probable dates are about B.C. 1700 and 1600 respectively.

About 17 feet above the base of City sub I we find the foundations of City II, in which Phoenician pottery first begins to appear (by the side of the 'Amorite' pottery). Passing this by, we come 3 feet above it to City III. In this a discovery of great interest was made: a small Assyrian tablet viz., about $2\frac{1}{2}$ in. by 2 in., was found, which upon examination proved not only to resemble those found at Tell el-Amarna, but to belong to the same series.[2]

---

[1] Bliss, p. 41 f. Not only is there no evidence that this pottery was distinctively 'Amorite', but Dr. Bliss (p. 41) expressly states that he uses the word not in an ethnological sense, but simply as a synonym for 'pre-Israelitish'.

[2] Petrie, *Egypt and Syria from the Tell el-Amarna Letters*, No. 235; Winckler, No. 219.

ROOMS IN A CASTLE AT MEGIDDO
To illustrate the appearance of an excavated site.
From *Tell el-Mutesellim* (1908), p. 17 (Fig. 12).

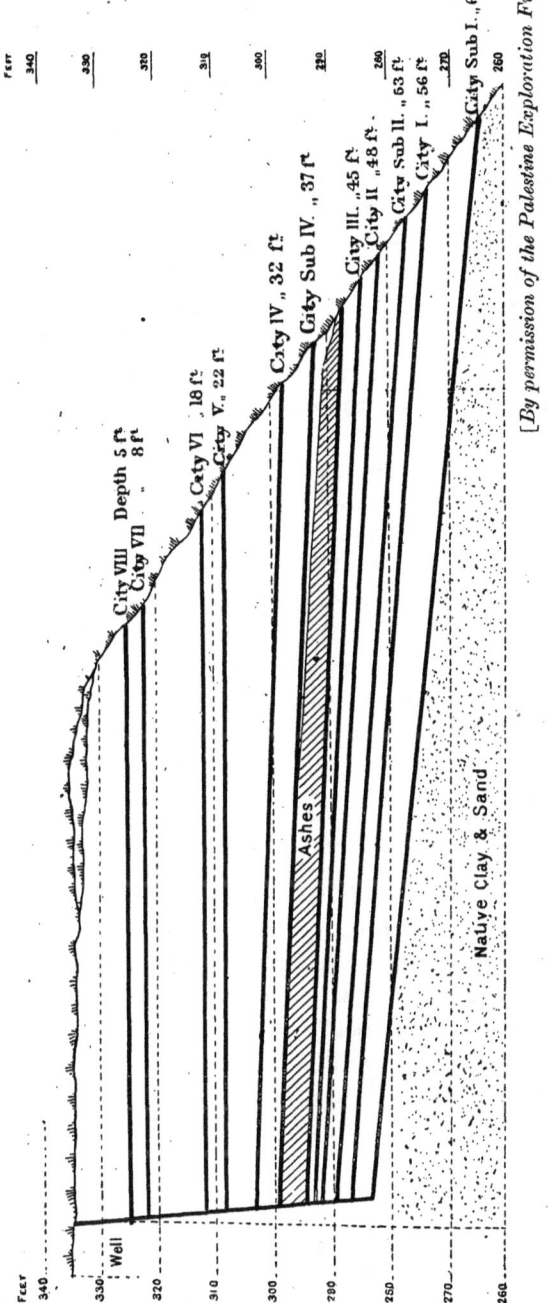

SECTION OF THE PART OF TELL EL-HESY EXCAVATED BY F. J. BLISS, SHOWING LEVELS OF CITY BASES, 1:300

[*By permission of the Palestine Exploration Fund.*]

The figures at the side indicate the heights in feet above the level of the sea. The Wâdy el-Hesy, at the base of the natural hill (of which only the top is here shown), is 220 feet above the sea.
From F. J. Bliss, *A Mound of Many Cities*, Plate II (p. 14).

It mentions one Zimrida, who, to judge from the locality, is not the Zimrida of Sidon, but the Zimrida, governor of Lachish, who, in one of the Tell el-Amarna letters,[1] promises to obey the orders of the Egyptian king, and who is also referred to in one of Abdi-ḥiba's letters[2] as conspired against by the enemies of the king. The tablet is unfortunately mutilated: but it apparently informs an unnamed general that Zimrida has been incited, and perhaps has even agreed, to call out the city against the king. The discovery of this tablet was important; for it fixes the date of City III, in the ruins of which it was found, to about B.C. 1400. Scarabs of the XVIIIth Dynasty appear in the same stratum, pointing to the same date. Above City III there comes a layer of ashes, varying from 3 to 7 feet in thickness, the origin of which is uncertain. Professor Petrie ascribes them to alkali-burners, who plied their trade on the deserted hill. Dr. Bliss thinks that they are the ashes of furnaces similar to one actually found in City II.[3] Professor Sayce regards them as the ashes 'left by charcoal-burners who squatted on the site before it was rebuilt'.[4] In any case the ashes do not indicate a long desolation, the pottery found above and below them being of the same type, and the scarabs of both Cities III and IV belonging to the same XVIIIth Dynasty. Above this layer of ashes are the remains of City IV, with scarabs of the XVIIIth and, at the top, of the XIXth Dynasty, pointing to the thirteenth century B.C., the probable period of the Hebrew conquest. At the top of City IV iron objects first appear: previously only bronze had been found. Here also a large symmetrical building, 58 feet square, containing many chambers, was excavated.[5] Numerous scarabs, bronze knives, and other objects, with lamps and other articles of Phoenician pottery, were also found.

We may pass rapidly over the remaining cities. The base of City V—or, if allowance be made for the cities sub I, II, and IV, the eighth city—is 22 feet from the top of the mound: in this also a large building was excavated, with pit-ovens near it, such as are used in Syria to-day.[6] Iron implements continue by the side of bronze. The characteristic pottery of the period now beginning (Cities V to VIII) was the Jewish, i.e. coarse copies of the older Phoenician types,[7] though Greek pottery begins to appear at the top of City VI. In the middle of the accumulated débris above City VI,

---

[1] Petrie, No. 98; Winckler, No. 217.
[2] Petrie, No. 234; Winckler, No. 181 (l. 42 f.).
[3] Bliss, p. 65 f.; see, for the furnace, pp. 47-51.
[4] Sayce, *Archaeology of the Cuneiform Inscriptions* (1907), p. 158.
[5] Bliss, pp. 72, 75.   [6] Ibid. p. 97.   [7] Ibid. p. 117.

SENNACHERIB RECEIVING THE SPOIL OF LACHISH

The middle part of a bas-relief now in the British Museum. The king is seated on his throne, with two eunuchs behind him holding fans, his warriors are standing in front, and the captives approach, crouching, on the left. In the parts of the bas-relief not here shown are seen the king's chariot, other warriors, and captives, &c. (The entire bas-relief is contained in the photographs from the British Museum, Nos. 433, 434, 436 of the Assyrian Series, published by Messrs. Mansell.)

From a Photograph by Messrs. Mansell.

and below the base of City VII, was found a limestone stand for a lamp, with a word consisting of seven rude Greek letters inscribed upon it, suggesting a date of about B.C. 500. In City VII fire-burnt brick has taken the place of sun-burnt brick;[1] and in City VIII were numerous pit-ovens, like those found in City V. In both City VII and City VIII specimens appeared of the polished red and black Greek pottery, with Greek figures painted upon them: the probable date of these would be about B.C. 500 and B.C. 400, respectively.[2] This rapid outline will, I hope, suffice to give some idea of the structure of this remarkable mound, and of the manner in which the succession of cities, built one after another upon the same site, can be determined by excavation, and their dates fixed, at least approximately, by the pottery and other objects found in them. The 65 feet which the mound now rises above the top of the natural hill contain the remains of not less than eleven cities, ranging in date from about B.C. 1700 to B.C. 400.

In all probability Tell el-Ḥesy is the site of the ancient Lachish. The name is not the same: but Lachish is known to have been a fortress; the situation would suit; and the manner in which Zimrida, who we know was governor of Lachish, is mentioned on the tablet found at Tell el-Ḥesy makes it highly probable that it was Lachish. In the Old Testament Lachish is first mentioned as a place taken by Joshua (Josh. x. 31 f.). It is next mentioned in the Chronicles (2 Chron. xi. 9) as a place built, i.e. fortified, by Rehoboam. When Sennacherib invaded Judah in 701, Lachish was one of the many fortified cities in Judah which he took (2 Kings xviii. 13, 14); and there is an interesting bas-relief, now in the British Museum,[3] representing the Assyrian king seated on his throne, and receiving the submission of Jewish captives, with the inscription, 'Sennacherib, king of multitudes, king of Assyria, seats himself upon a lofty throne, and receives the spoil of the city of Lachish.' If Tell el-Ḥesy be really Lachish, it would be the strong walls of City VI (10–12 feet thick)[4] which the Assyrian king succeeded in forcing. Sennacherib made the captured fortress for some time his headquarters: Hezekiah's envoys came thither with large presents to ask of him terms of peace; and thence it was that he dispatched

---

[1] Ibid. p. 108. [2] Ibid. pp. 121 f., 136 f., 139.
[3] Assyrian Saloon, No. 28. See the shilling *Guide to the Babylonian and Assyrian Antiquities in the British Museum* (1900), p. 28. This book contains a very large amount of interesting information respecting cuneiform inscriptions preserved in the Museum, and their contents.
[4] Bliss, p. 99.

Rabshakeh to demand the surrender of Jerusalem (2 Kings xviii. 14–16, 17 ff.). A century later (Jer. xxxiv. 7) it is mentioned as one of the fortresses attacked by Nebuchadnezzar.

Let me now pass to speak of the excavations at Gezer. Forty years ago the site of Gezer was unknown. Its site was discovered by that sound and brilliant French archaeologist, M. Clermont-Ganneau. In 1871 M. Clermont-Ganneau found it stated by a mediaeval Arabic author, Mujir ed-Din, that the sounds of a *mêlée* at a place called Khoulda could be heard at *Tell ej-Jezer*. The site of Khoulda was known; so the next time that M. Ganneau visited it, in 1874, he inquired of the inhabitants whether there was a Tell ej-Jezer near to it: they replied that there was, and pointed

[*By permission of the Palestine Exploration Fund.*]

BOUNDARY-INSCRIPTIONS OF GEZER

From copies made on the spot by M. Lecomte (see Clermont-Ganneau's *Archaeological Researches in Palestine*, 1896, published by the Palestine Exploration Fund, ii. 228, and 225–6). The Aramaic part of the upper inscription is inverted: but this inscription (like the other) is carved on a horizontal surface of rock, so that half of it can be read from each side.

out the Tell to him, about three miles to the north. It lies some twenty-eight miles north-east of Tell el-Ḥesy, and nineteen miles west-north-west of Jerusalem. This, however, was not all. M. Ganneau heard that an inscription was to be seen near the Tell: so proceeding with workmen to the point indicated, about 5,600 feet east of the centre of the Tell, he soon discovered on a rock an inscription, about six feet in length, written partly in Greek, and partly in Aramaic, ΑΛΚΙΟ[Υ], תחם גזר, i.e. '*Of Alkios. Boundary of Gezer.*' Soon afterwards two other rocks were found in a line north and south of the first, at the same distance from the Tell, similarly inscribed; and in 1898 Père Lagrange found a fourth. Alkios was presumably a Greek governor of the place; the words 'Boundary of Gezer'

View of Tell ej-Jezer from the South

demonstrated that the spot was really the site of the ancient Gezer. M. Ganneau, in a study on the subject,[1] showed also that it was the Mont Gisart often mentioned in histories of the Crusades. George Adam Smith, long before the site had been excavated, perceived its strategical importance. Standing near the end of a ridge of hills, and overlooking the plain towards Ramleh and Joppa, it forms at once 'a very strong post, and striking landmark. Within sight of every Egyptian and every Assyrian invasion of the land, Gezer has also seen Alexander pass by, and the legions of Rome in unusual flight, and the armies of the Cross struggle, waver, and give way, and Napoleon come and go'.[2] Gezer is first actually mentioned in history as one of the cities taken by Thothmes III (c. 1475 B.C.); but scarabs and other Egyptian objects found in it testify to a very considerable trade and communication with Egypt in the time of the XIIth and XIIIth Dynasties, some 500 years earlier, and show that it was already then a place of some importance. We hear of Gezer next in the Tell el-Amarna Letters, three of which[3] are written by its governor, Yapaḥi. In these letters Yapaḥi declares that he is hard pressed by the *Sa-gas*[4]—a people sometimes identified with the Ḥabiri, and certainly allied to them—that his brother has rebelled, and joined them, and that he is in urgent need of help from the Egyptian king; and Abdi-ḥiba, of Jerusalem, complains of the disloyalty of the Gezerites. Gezer is mentioned next by Merenptah (c. 1230 B.C.) in the inscription already quoted (p. 39), 'Gezer is taken.' In the traditions of the Israelite conquest, its king and the men with him, coming to the help of Lachish, are said to have been all slain by Joshua (Josh. x. 33).[5] Its Canaanite inhabitants, however, were not driven out, but reduced to servitude (Josh. xvi. 10 = Jud. i. 29). They remained in possession of it till the time of Solomon, when, we are told (1 Kings ix. 16),

---

[1] *Recueil d'Archéologie*, i. (1888), 351-92.

[2] *Historical Geography of the Holy Land*, 1894, p. 216 f.

[3] Petrie, *Egypt and Syria*, &c., Nos. 236-8; Winckler, Nos. 204-6.

[4] See p. 34, note.

[5] In Joshua xxi. 21 (=1 Chron. vi. 67) Gezer is also said to have been a 'Levitical city'. The 'Levitical cities', however, are mentioned only in the late priestly sections of the Hexateuch (Lev. xxv. 32-4; Num. xxxv. 1-8; Joshua xiv. 4; xxi), and the Book of Chronicles (1 Chron. vi. 57-81, transcribed from Joshua xxi; xiii. 2; 2 Chron. xi. 14; xxxi. 19): the institution expresses an *ideal*, and it is uncertain how far, if at all, it was ever carried into practice (cf. Hastings's *Dict. of the Bible*, v. 717ᵇ). There were certainly, in the age of Moses and Joshua, no 'Levites' in the sense in which the term is used (as opposed to 'priests') in the priestly sections of the Hexateuch; and Gezer, besides (see above), was not occupied by Israelites at all till the reign of Solomon.

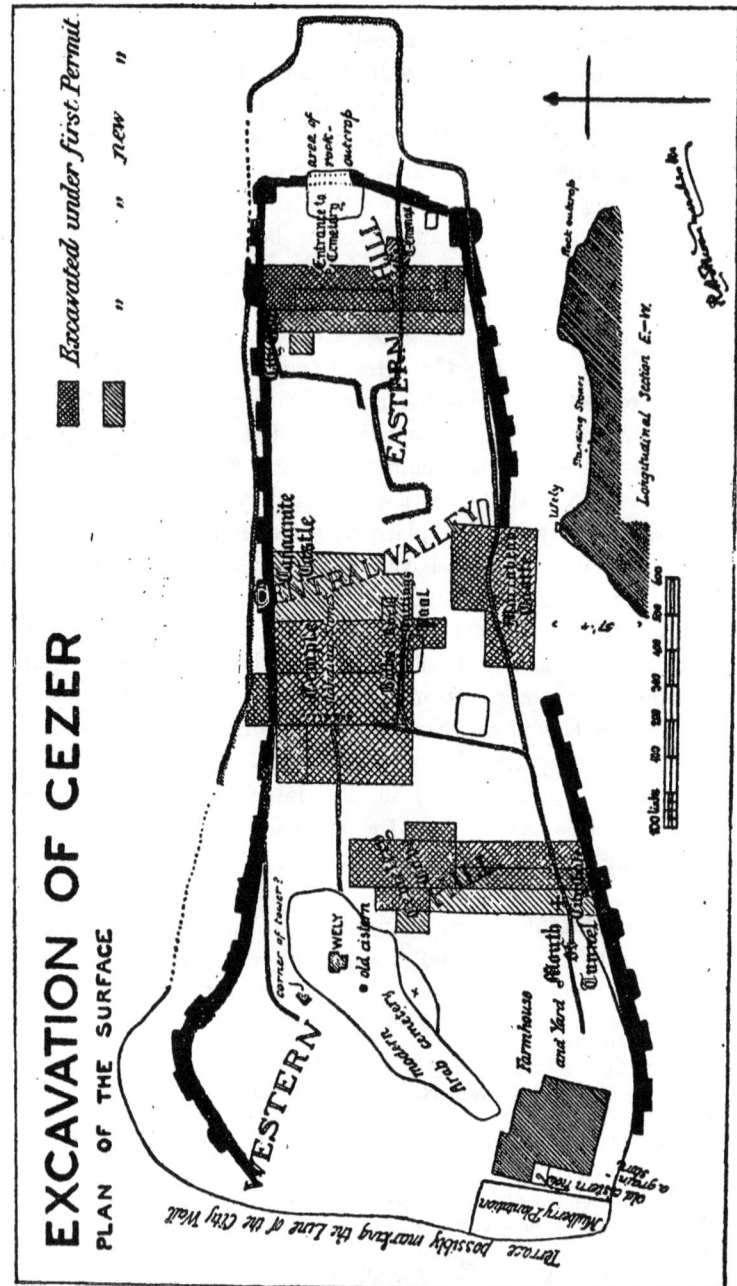

[*By permission of the Palestine Exploration Fund.*

PLAN OF GEZER, AS EXPOSED BY EXCAVATION.
From the *Quarterly Statement*, 1908, facing p. 1.

the then king of Egypt attacked and burnt Gezer, slew the Canaanites in it, and gave the site as a marriage-portion to his daughter, whom Solomon had taken as his wife. The hopes once entertained that the ashes left when the city was burnt by Pharaoh, or a tablet mentioning the name of Solomon's father-in-law, might be found, have, however, up to the present time, not been realized. We hear nothing more of Gezer till the times of the Maccabees, when Bacchides, after his defeat by Jonathan, fortified it (161 B.C.), to 'vex the Jews' (1 Macc. ix. 52). In 143, Simon, 'the great high-priest and captain of the Jews,' took Gezer with an 'engine of war', expelled the Syrians from it, purified the houses in which there had been idols, placed in it loyal Israelites, and built in it a palace for himself (1 Macc. xiii. 43-8), to which I shall have occasion to refer again.

Mr. Macalister was engaged in his excavations at Gezer from June 14, 1902, to Aug. 30, 1905. The period for which the Turkish government had granted permission for them then expired: but, a new firman having been obtained, they were resumed on March 18, 1907, and are still [1908] being carried on. The liberality of the Turkish government in granting such firmans cannot be too warmly acknowledged; and the results, both in this and in other cases, have been a series of most important discoveries, of the greatest value for the advance of archaeological and historical knowledge.

The remains of Gezer lie a few yards east of the modern village Abu-Shusheh, forming a long low mound, resting on two hills, an east and a west hill, with a depression between them. On the east hill there are stratified buildings representing four successive occupations. The depression between them exhibits three other strata, one preceding, and two following, the four represented by the east hill.[1]

The two lowest of these strata are earlier than anything found at Tell el-Ḥesy, and belong in fact to the Neolithic age.[2] Mr. Macalister's first excavations showed that at that time Gezer was occupied by an aboriginal non-Semitic race, of small stature, between five feet four inches and five feet seven inches in height, who lived in caves, or in rude huts of wood and stone, and who (as was shown by the remains of calcined bones, and a blackened chimney) cremated their dead in a cave arranged for the purpose, in which, in accordance with a widely diffused practice, they placed food-vessels for the use of the deceased. Here is a plan of this Neolithic burial-cave. It is about

---

[1] QS. (i.e. *Quarterly Statement of the Palestine Exploration Fund*) 02. 319, 364; 03. 8 f., 13 (Table of strata at Gezer; cf. 03. 286-9).

[2] QS. 03. 286.

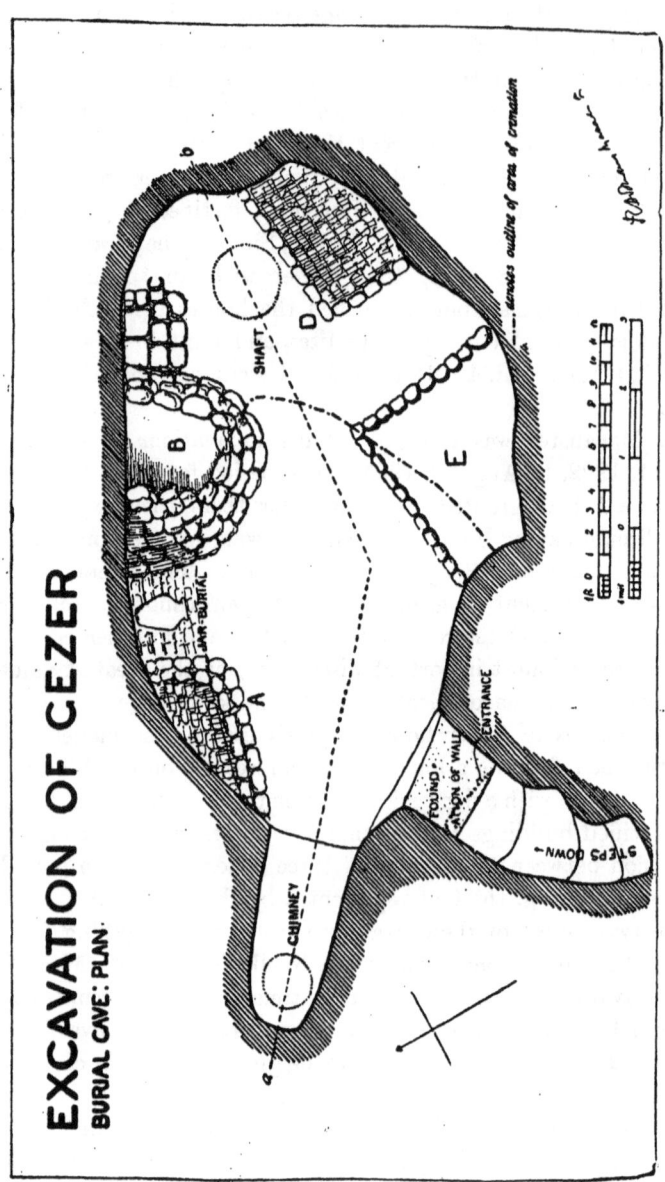

[*By permission of the Palestine Exploration Fund.*

PLAN OF THE NEOLITHIC BURIAL-CAVE.
From the *Quarterly Statement*, 1902, p. 371.

[*By permission of the Palestine Exploration Fund.*

JAR FROM THE BURIAL-CAVE, CONTAINING AN INFANT'S BONES

The rule is one foot in length. The jar was found at the spot marked in the plan of the cave between *A* and *B*. From this being the only infant buried in a jar, found in the cave, it is supposed to have been a sacrifice, offered perhaps when the cave was first adapted for burial (ibid., p. 352). Cf. below, p. 68.

From the *Quarterly Statement*, 1902, p. 361.

CUP-MARKS IN ROCK-SURFACE ABOVE THREE LARGE CAVES

From *Bible Side-Lights from the Mound of Gezer*, p. 46 (cf. *Quarterly Statement*, 1904, p. 111).

[*By permission of the Palestine Exploration Fund.*]

thirty feet long by twenty-four broad. A B C D E are platforms, or enclosures, of flat stones, supposed to have been the graves of persons of distinction.[1] The entire settlement was surrounded by an earth rampart, about six feet high, and six feet thick, strengthened on the interior by a stone wall two feet thick, and with a curving exterior protected by a facing of stone [2]—very different from the massive stone defences constructed in later times. In one part of this stratum, on a large rock surface, some ninety feet square, there were found a large number (eighty-three) of cup-marks, some large, some small, artificially cut in the rock, with three large caves underneath, and an orifice, too narrow to admit a man, leading down into it. It has been supposed that these cup-marks served some religious purpose, and that the orifice was used as a shoot conveying downwards blood, or other objects, as offerings to underground deities.[3] This view received afterwards some confirmation from the discovery at Taanach of a rock-altar, communicating by winding stone stairs, and also by a channel or conduit, both cut out in the rock, with two large caves underneath.[4] Perhaps the rock surface found at Gezer was the 'high place' of the Neolithic cave-dwellers.[5]

The pottery found in these caves was of the rudest description, moulded by hand, and sometimes decorated with roughly painted red or white lines. Metal seems to have been unknown. Flint is the material used for cutting-implements, great dexterity being shown in flaking off fine long and sharp knives from the core, though tools of rougher make were commonly found sufficient. The probable date of these Troglodyte dwellings is before 2000 B.C. The domestic animals certainly known to the Troglodytes were the sheep, cow, pig, and goat: the bones of these, and also of such birds as the stork, were fashioned into various implements, especially pins and prickers, probably for perforating skins. Grindstones show that the people practised agriculture of a sort, and were acquainted with the art of axe-grinding. The rotary grinder, however, is unknown,

---

[1] *QS.* 02. 351 f.

[2] *QS.* 03. 113, 116 (section); or Vincent, *Canaan d'après l'exploration récente* (1907), p. 30. This important work of Père Vincent's is practically an exhaustive account of the results of excavation in Palestine up to the time at which it was written (the Preface is dated Nov. 1906). It contains a large number of illustrations.

[3] *QS.* 03. 317 (plan of rock-surface, with cups and caves), 318 f. In the cave, underneath the orifice, were found a number of pig-bones (p. 321), suggesting that the pig was the animal sacrificed in these rites (*QS.* 04. 113; Macalister, *Bible Side-Lights from the Mound of Gezer*, p. 48).

[4] See below, p. 83; also p. 67.   [5] *QS.* 04. 112 f.

the rubbing-stone being the variety in use.[1] Whether the people who inhabited these caves had any connexion with the Horites, the pre-Semitic population of Edom (Gen. xxxvi. 20–30), is very problematical.[2] It is true, caves in the mountain-sides were used as dwellings in Petra to a much later period: but there is at present absolutely no evidence connecting the Gezer caves with the Horites. Several other caves which had been originally Troglodyte dwellings were also discovered in different parts of Gezer, which, as they were used afterwards for other purposes, will be referred to again.[3]

In 1907, while a new trench was being dug on the west hill, just west of the city gate, there was found, when the rock was reached, a large entrance to what at first appeared to be a pool; but upon

THE RUBBING-STONE

From *Tell el-Mutesellim*, p. 64. The oval-shaped stone in the middle has a flat under-surface, which is rubbed to and fro by hand over the rectangular table of stone underneath, on which the corn is spread.

The ordinary rotary grinder, or handmill, consisted—as it consists still in Palestine,—of two circular slabs of stone, 18 inches or 2 feet in diameter, the lower one being fixed on the ground, and the upper one being turned round upon it by a woman (Exod. xi. 5), or two women (Matt. xxiv. 41), kneeling or sitting beside it.

the explorers penetrating further, it was found to be the entrance to a long and remarkable subterranean gallery or tunnel, descending by eighty steps, and leading ultimately to a large cave containing a spring of water. This tunnel was altogether 219 feet long and for the greater part of its length 23 feet high and 12 feet 10 inches

---

[1] *QS.* 04. 113 f.

[2] The heading 'The Horites' of chap. ii. in Mr. Macalister's *Bible Side-Lights from the Mound of Gezer* is unfortunate; for it suggests an identity which is not claimed even by Mr. Macalister himself (p. 42).

[3] *QS.* 07. 186. See below, pp. 54, 56.

SUBTERRANEAN TUNNEL FOUND AT GEZER 53

across, but for the last third of the course, when the rock became harder, its dimensions contracted considerably. The water, which the tunnel ultimately reached, was 94 feet below the surface of the rock, and 130 feet below the present surface of the soil.[1] The tunnel appears to have been excavated before 2000 B.C., and to have been abandoned between 1400 and 1200 B.C. It is a remarkable work for such an early date; and, as Père Vincent has remarked,[2] cannot but enhance our estimate of the engineering capabilities, and, indirectly, of the civilization generally, of the race who produced it. The object of the tunnel was, presumably, to ensure a supply of water for the city, in the event of a siege.

To the same early period belongs also a curious pottery model of a shrine, found in a deep stratum associated with remains pointing to 2000 B.C., which, though only partially preserved, showed clearly the remains of a broken figure seated upon it.[3]

Since these lectures were delivered, a further discovery has been made, which also takes us back to the Neolithic age.[4] Under thirty feet of débris, representing eight strata, there was found, namely, another cave hollowed out in the rock, a little west of the mouth of the great tunnel, just described; and on the rock walls of this cave there were carved a number of rude drawings of animals. The drawings consist of little more than combinations of rectangular lines; but they are clearly intended to represent animals—mostly cows, sometimes, perhaps, stags, and buffaloes. 'These drawings,' writes Mr. Macalister, 'whatever their origin, are beyond all question the oldest works of art that Palestine has yet produced. They strangely recall the Palaeolithic sketches that have been found in various places; but I hesitate to commit myself to the theory that they are actually of a date so remote, although there is plenty of evidence for the existence of Palaeolithic man within five miles of Gezer.'

The third and fourth strata, which lie next above those in which the Troglodyte caves were found, are shown by the scarabs contained in them to belong to the period from the XIIth to the XIXth Dynasty,[5] i.e. from probably c. 2000 to 1200 B.C. Deposits dating from the earlier part of this period were found in 1905 on the west hill in an extensive series of caves—consisting of ten separate

---

[1] QS. 08. 15 ff., 96 ff. [2] QS. 08. 222 f. [3] QS. 08. 21 f.
[4] QS. 08. 213-18 (with plan and illustration); 273 (withdrawing the opinion, expressed before, that the drawings date from the Palaeolithic age).
[5] QS. 04. 245.

chambers connected together by passages—originally excavated in pre-Semitic times[1] as dwellings for the Neolithic Troglodytes, but afterwards used by their successors as cemeteries. The people buried in these caves—for the dead were no longer cremated— were a Semitic race, of stronger build than the Troglodytes, 5 feet 7 inches to 5 feet 11 inches in height. The style of burial is thoroughly Egyptian, save that the bodies are not embalmed. The tombs contained many objects deposited in them for the use of the deceased.[2] The scarabs found in these caves are in sufficient abundance to fix the date of the interments to the period of the XIIth Egyptian Dynasty.[3] There seems thus to have been at the time of this dynasty (according to Breasted,[4] 2000–1788 B.C.) a settled Egyptian colony or population in South Palestine, about the coast-road to Syria, keeping up, to judge from the style of burial at Gezer, and from two funerary inscriptions found there, Egyptian customs.[5] That the bodies found in these cave-cemeteries are not embalmed is, Mr. Griffith states, in agreement with contemporary usage in Egypt itself. Of Babylonian influence there is, on the contrary, at this period no trace.[6] Elsewhere scarabs belonging to the period of the Hyksos kings (XIV–XVII Dynasties) were found: these are of interest, as testifying to intercourse at this time between Egypt and Palestine, of which previously nothing was known.[7] Other sepulchre-caves resembling those just mentioned were discovered afterwards: one, used originally as a cistern, but converted by the inhabitants of the third stratum (i.e. of the second city on the eastern hill) into a burial-cave, containing fifteen skeletons and various bronze objects buried with them[8]; the others belonging to the period of the XVIIIth Dynasty: one of these contained a cartouche of Thothmes III.[9]

The city at this time was surrounded by a substantial stone wall, the remains of which show that it must have been 10 to 11 feet thick: it is composed of 'large irregular hammer-trimmed stones, ranging from 1 foot 7 inches to 2 feet in length and height, roughly chipped to shape, with the joints very wide and nearly all packed with smaller stones'; and it appears to have had 'long narrow towers of small projection at intervals of 90 feet in its

---

[1] QS. 05. 209 ff. (with plan of the caves).
[2] QS. 03. 286, 05. 316, 04. 324 ff.   [3] QS. 05. 314.
[4] *Hist. of Egypt* (1905), pp. 22, 598. Similarly W. Max Müller in the *Encycl. Biblica*, ii. 1237, note 3. Petrie places the dynasty earlier.
[5] QS. 06. 122 (F. Ll. Griffith). Cf. 03. 37, 05. 317.
[6] QS. 05. 316.   [7] QS. 04. 245.
[8] QS. 03. 12-20, with plan.   [9] QS. 07. 256.

THE EXCAVATION OF GEZER IN PROGRESS
From *Bible Side-Lights from the Mound of Gezer*, p. 8.
[*By permission of the Palestine Exploration Fund.*

course'. On its south side was a massive gateway, 42 feet long, and with a passage 9 feet wide, standing between two towers, 28 feet long, and still 16 feet high, composed of rude rubble masonry, faced with sun-burnt bricks, measuring on an average 15 inches by 11 inches by 4 inches. The passage-way was roughly paved with stones. This south gateway affords indications enabling us to fix the date of the wall of which it formed part. Above the towers just spoken of were houses containing scarabs, beads, pottery, &c., all pointing to the time of Amenhotep III (c. 1400 B.C.). It may be inferred that both the gate, and the wall to which it belonged, were then ruined and useless; and the depth of the strata in which the wall lies makes it probable that it was built 1,000 years earlier. Thus Gezer for 1,000 years or more before 1500 B.C. was a large and strongly fortified city.[1] The houses, however, were small, and show no attempt at decoration. The streets were crooked and narrow, and many end in blank walls: there are no traces of continuous thoroughfares.[2] During the early Semitic period, ending with the invasion of the Hebrews, bronze, or sometimes copper, continues to be the normal metal, iron being still absent.[3]

After about 1400 B.C. a larger wall—called, for distinction from the wall just mentioned, the outer wall—was built.[4] This wall, which is on a higher level than the previous wall, will have been built after the older wall had become useless,[5] i.e. at about the same time as the houses above this, just referred to, or c. 1400 B.C. It measured on the average 14 feet in thickness, and the stones of which it was composed were large and well-shaped: on the whole, however, the masonry is not as good as that of the first wall. It contained thirty towers, some internal, others external, the latter projecting—as a rule, but not universally—alternately 3 and 12 feet beyond the face of the wall.[6] Two of these towers are composed of the same fairly large stones, dressed roughly with the hammer only, set in mud, and with the joints and corners packed with small field stones, as the rest of the wall, and are bonded into it: the remaining twenty-eight towers are of smaller stones, well-chiselled, and dressed to a truly rectangular shape. It is inferred, therefore, that sections of the original wall were removed at these points, and the well-built square towers inserted in the cleared spaces. Further, near the west end of the north side, for a length of about

---

[1] QS. 03. 114, 214 f.; 04. 203-6; cf. 05. 28 f.
[2] QS. 04. 115; cf. the plan, p. 116.   [3] Ibid. 119.
[4] Ibid. 200.   [5] QS. 05. 28
[6] QS. 02. 320; 04. 203; 05. 29 f.

56 CANAAN AS KNOWN THROUGH EXCAVATION

150 feet, the masonry, though inferior to that of the towers, is of the same general character, and in Mr. Macalister's opinion contemporary. Mr. Macalister infers that the wall was for this length breached by some enemy, and afterwards repaired and strengthened by the addition of the well-built towers just referred to. He conjectures that this repair and strengthening of the wall was effected by Pharaoh, after Gezer had been taken and burnt by him, and given as a dowry to his daughter, Solomon's queen.[1] This wall served as the defence for the city built over the brick-faced towers, and for two other cities that overlaid this—three in all: it thus lasted in use for some 1,400 years, from c. 1500 to 100 B.C.[2]

Relics of the same period were also found in two Troglodyte caves, discovered in 1907 on the west side of the east hill. One of these had afterwards been made into a cistern, in the XIXth Egyptian Dynasty, as was shown by the pottery in it, which was of the same type as that in City sub IV at Tell el-Ḥesy: the other had been adapted in the first Semitic period as a burial-place, and was a century or two afterwards rediscovered by cistern-diggers, who left in it pottery dating from about 1300 B.C.[3]

Above the second of these caves there were found at the same time the foundations (see plan and view in *QS.* 07. 192, 195) of what must have been a Canaanite castle, the most elaborate building as yet discovered at Gezer. The inner city wall—which is at least 1,000 years older than the castle, and had already been superseded by the outer wall when the castle was built—was adopted as the north side of the structure. It is built round one of the internal towers of this wall. The walls were from 3 to 9 feet thick; and the objects found in or about the building point to a date in the thirteenth century B.C.

The period of the fourth stratum was one in which the worship of the Phoenician and Canaanite goddess 'Ashtōreth (or 'Ashtart [4]), the female consort of Baal, often mentioned in Phoenician inscriptions,[5] seems to have been very popular: for terra-cotta plaques bearing figures, as it seems, of this goddess in relief in an interesting

---

[1] *QS.* 05. 29–31.   [2] Ibid. 28.   [3] *QS.* 07. 188, 190 f.

[4] The Greek form *Astartè* suggests this as the ancient pronunciation of the Phoenician and (unvocalized) Hebrew עשתרת.

[5] See particulars of the character of this goddess, and the wide extent of her worship, in Hastings's *Dict. of the Bible*, s. v. (i. 167–71). In the Old Testament see 1 Kings xi. 5, 33; 2 Kings xxiii. 13; and in the *plural* form, 'Ashtārōth'—no doubt, denoting the local Ashtōreths, like the 'Baālim', the local Baals—Judges ii. 13; x. 6; 1 Sam. vii. 3, 4; xii. 10; xxxi. 10 [but read here the sing. 'Ashtōreth' for 'the Ashtārōth'; there is no article in the Heb.].

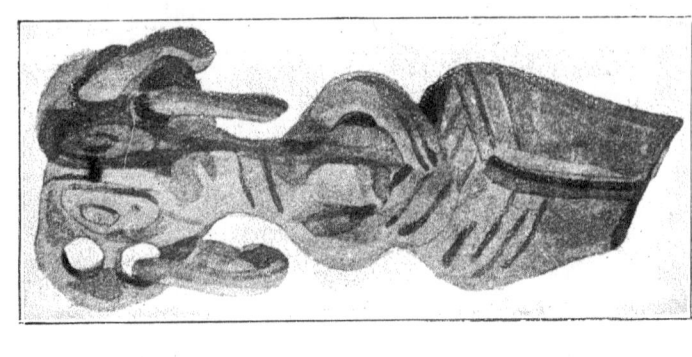

3. Astarte Figure, of peculiar type, from Taanach

From *Tell Taʿannek*, p. 80.

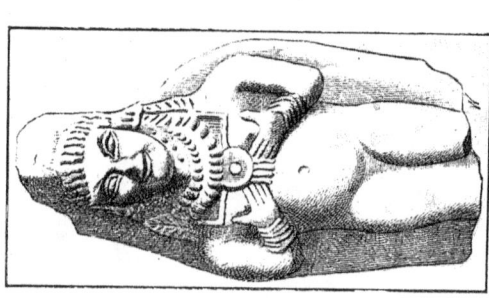

2. Terra-cotta Figure of Astarte from Cyprus

Height, 8 inches.

From Perrot and Chipiez, *History of Art in Phoenicia and Cyprus*, ii. p. 52. In the original, *Histoire de l'art dans l'antiquité*, Tome iii (1885), p. 450, Fig. 321.

1. Clay Figure of Astarte from Taanach

Height, 7 inches.

From Sellin's *Tell Taʿannek* (1904), p. 45.

FIGURES OF ASTARTE FOUND IN CANAAN 57

variety of types, were found in large numbers in the fourth stratum, and hardly, if at all, elsewhere.[1] The only one of which an illustration is given by Mr. Macalister is of an exceptional Egyptian type.[2] What are doubtless representations of the same goddess have also been discovered in other parts of Palestine. Thus Dr. Bliss found in City sub IV at Tell el-Ḥesy a small pottery figure of a female, of a Phoenician type, to all appearance representing Ashtōreth.[3] At Taanach Professor Sellin found a number (nineteen) of clay figures, also apparently Astarte, represented as an undraped female, the hands holding the breasts, with a high tiara on the head, a curl, necklace, girdle, and anklet.[4] This resembles the usual Phoenician type, as the illustration opposite of a terra-cotta figure found in Cyprus will sufficiently show. In a house belonging to the Israelite period, Professor Sellin also came across one of a very peculiar type, with huge ears and ear-rings[5]; some closely resembling these have, however, been found in Cyprus[6] and at Zinjirli (near Aleppo).

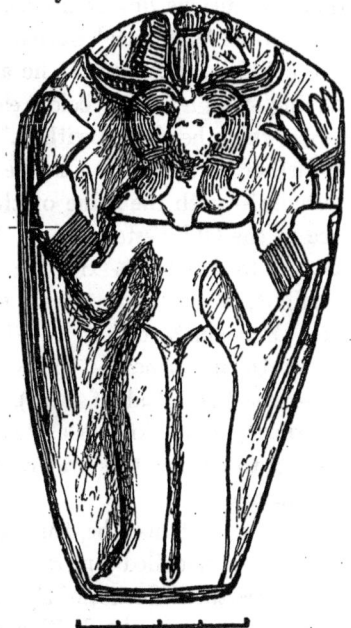

1 inch.

[*By permission of the Palestine Exploration Fund.*]

ASTARTE-PLAQUE, OF EGYPTIAN TYPE, FROM GEZER

Height, 3 inches. From the *Quarterly Statement*, 1904, p. 15.

[1] *QS.* 04. 15, 118. It is difficult to think that Mr. Macalister is right in identifying (*QS.* 05. 270 f.) these figures with the 'teraphim' of the Old Testament; for these, to judge from 1 Sam. xix. 13, 16, must have been much larger. Images representing probably household gods in a more general sense, and not specifically teraphim, were however found in numbers at Gezer (*Side-Lights*, p. 106). Cf. the tutelary bronze image found at Taanach, fixed to the wall of a fallen Canaanite house (*c.* 1300 B.C.), amid the remains of the family who had perished in the accident—the mother with her knife in her hand, and food-vessels round about, and with her ornaments and amulets still in their places on her skeleton (*Nachlese*, Fig. 20; Vincent, p. 163, with illustration; *Side-Lights*, p. 10).   [2] *QS.* 04. 15 (=Vincent, p. 160).

[3] *A Mound of Many Cities*, p. 68; Vincent, p. 165.

[4] *Tell Ta'annek*, pp. 45, 106. See the Plate opposite, No. 1. Perhaps (Sellin) each city had its own type of Astarte-figure, and this was the Taanach type; it was found at Taanach in strata dating from 1600 to 800 B.C.

[5] *Ta'annek*, pp. 80, 106; Vincent, p. 165. See the Plate opposite, No. 3.

[6] See the illustrations in Perrot and Chipiez, *Hist. of Art in Phoenicia and*

In the sixth stratum at Gezer, also, Mr. Macalister found a small bronze statuette, 4½ in. high, representing an undraped female, which, from the curious downward coiling projections by the ears, he supposes to be Ashtōreth [1] Karnaim [2], i.e. 'Ashtōreth of the two horns', or the 'Horned Astarte': he also found a plaque with projections running straight down below each ear, and then curved round outwards, which he classed with it.[3] Till this identification is confirmed by further evidence, it must be regarded as doubtful. 'Ashterōth-Karnaim'—with the name of the goddess in the *plural*—occurs only once in the Old Testament, as the name of a *place* in Bashan, on the east of Jordan (Gen. xiv. 5); and its interpretation is uncertain: it might, for instance, mean simply Ashtaroth of (i.e. near) the place Karnaim [4], or, if we discard the Massoretic vocalization, Ashtōreth of Karnaim—the whole being the name of a place, like Baal-Peor (i.e. Baal of Peor).[5] There *may*, no doubt, have been a horned goddess known as 'Ashtōreth Karnaim'; but we are not entitled to assume this on the strength of the ambiguous expression in Gen. xiv. 5.

However that may be, the variety of Astarte types is interesting. Some seem modelled on Babylonian, others on Phoenician types; a few show the influence of Egyptian art.[6] The history of the cult of 'Ashtart' is remarkable.[7] The Phoenician goddess is the link connecting the Assyrian Ishtar with the Greek Aphrodite. Born originally in the far east, she was born again for the Greeks from the foam (ἀφρός) of Cyprus: and once brought under touch of the creative genius of Greece, her character was transformed; she furnished art

Cyprus, ii. p. 150 (in the original, p. 553, Fig. 375), and in Heuzey's *Figurines antiques du Musée du Louvre*, Plate IV, Fig. 5 (with the same huge ears, but without ear-rings). For the statement about the figures from Zinjirli, see Ohnefalsch-Richter, *Cyprus* (1893), i. p. 33.

[1] Mr. Macalister writes by error 'Ashtaroth'—the *plural* form, which, moreover, with a genitive following, would become 'Ashteroth', as it is in Gen. xiv. 5.

[2] *QS.* 03. 226 (illustration), 227. Vincent, p. 164.

[3] *QS.* 03. 228 (illustration). Cf. the similarly shaped projections on an Astarte found by Sellin at Taanach (see the Plate opposite). Père Vincent, however, doubts (p. 164, note) whether in this case the projections represent horns; he thinks that they rather represent long curls.

[4] See Hastings's *Dict. of the Bible*, i. 167ᵃ.

[5] See G. F. Moore in the *Enc. Bibl.* i. 335 with note 3, 336 note 3; or, more fully, in the American *Journal of Biblical Literature*, xvi. (1897), p. 157, where he compares the Punic Baal-Karnain, i.e. 'Baal of the two horns *or* peaks', so called because his sanctuary (near Carthage) lay on a mountain formed by two very sharp peaks, separated by a deep gorge.

[6] See more fully Vincent, pp. 159-65 (with illustrations).

[7] See the writer's article in Hastings's *Dict. of the Bible*, i. 168-71.

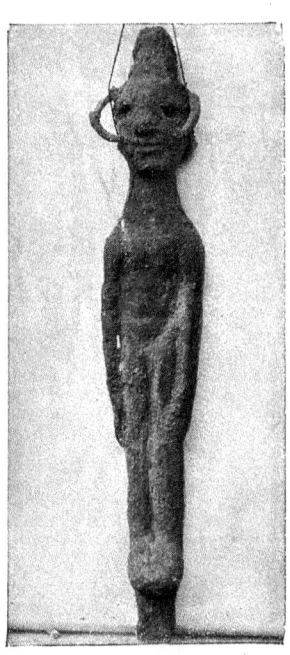

POSSIBLE HORNED ASTARTE FROM GEZER

From *Side-Lights from the Mound of Gezer*, p. 96
(cf. *Quarterly Statement*, 1903, p. 226).

CLAY FIGURE OF ASTARTE FOUND AT TAANACH
Height, 4⅓ inches.

From *Tell Ta'annek*, p. 50.

DIFFERENT TYPES OF ASTARTE FIGURES

with its most attractive ideals of female grace and beauty; she became even the personification of the all-pervading and vital force of nature.[1] In figures of her found in Cyprus she is often represented as holding a dove in her bosom; in others, she assumes a pose which has even been supposed to have been the original of the Venus of Medici. The time has come for the publication, in some readily accessible work, of illustrations exhibiting side by side the different Astarte-types at present known—Babylonian and Phoenician, not less than Canaanite:[2] perhaps in the near future some archaeologist interested in the subject may undertake this.

The influence of Aegean art is also very evident in much of the pottery of the same period.[3]

---

[1] Compare the invocation to her, beginning 'Diva Astarte, hominum deorumque vis, vita, salus', placed in the mouth of an Athenian woman by Plautus (*Mercator*, IV. vi. 825 ff.).

[2] See references—collected before the discoveries recently made in Palestine—to works in which Babylonian and Phoenician examples may be seen, ibid., pp. 170-1. It may suffice here to mention Perrot and Chipiez, *History of Art in Phoenicia and Cyprus*, i. figs. 20, 142-4, ii. figs. 15, 46-8, 98, 103-6, 141, 274 (in the original, *Histoire de l'art dans l'antiquité*, Tome iii., figs. 20, 142-4, 291, 322-4, 374, 379-82, 417, 550). For a new type, discovered quite recently at Gezer, see *QS.* 09. 15, with the accompanying description. It is to be hoped that Mr. Macalister will not confine the collection of Astarte-types, which he promises (ibid., p. 14) for his forthcoming memoir, to those found at Gezer only.

[3] *QS.* 03. 287; cf. Vincent, p. 326 ff.

III. CANAAN, AS KNOWN THROUGH INSCRIPTIONS AND EXCAVATION (*continued*)

I WAS speaking at the end of my last Lecture of the third and fourth strata at Gezer, representing the period before the Hebrew invasion of Palestine. The most interesting discovery belonging to this period was that of a large High Place. Before describing this I will, however, mention briefly what we learn about High Places from the Old Testament, and describe one discovered a few years ago elsewhere.

In the Old Testament mention is often made of the *bāmāh*, or high place, as a place of sacrifice. The fullest particulars are given in 1 Sam. ix. Saul, engaged in the search for his father's lost asses, wishes to consult the seer, Samuel: the city in which Samuel dwells, probably Ramah, lies on the slope of a hill: at the entrance to the city he meets girls going down to draw water at the foot of the hill, who tell him that Samuel is about to go up to the high place on the hill above the city, to preside at a sacrificial meal. Saul meets Samuel just as he is leaving the city for this purpose; at his invitation he goes up with him to the high place to the chamber in which, after the sacrifice, the sacred meal takes place, and a party of about thirty guests sit down and partake of it. It is a remarkable and interesting picture: clearly at this time there was nothing illegitimate in sacrifice and worship at such a place. Afterwards, however, on account of the heathen rites in vogue at many of these high places, they were proscribed by legislators and prophets; and Hezekiah and Josiah both exerted themselves to abolish them. The high places of Israel and Judah are often alluded to in the books of Kings and the prophets: we may infer indeed from the terms in which they are spoken of that every city and village had one (2 Kings xvii. 9, 11; xxiii. 8; Ezek. vi. 6). We know also from Isaiah's prophecy on Moab (xv. 2; xvi. 12) that there were high places in Moab: the high place which Mesha, in his inscription (*c.* 800 B.C.), states that he made for Chemosh, the national deity of Moab, may be one of those alluded to by Isaiah. We could infer from the Old Testament that they were sacred places, with altars [1] on which sacrifice was offered,[2] and

[1] See 1 Kings iii. 4 (at Gibeon); Hos. x. 8 (at Bethel); 2 Kings xxiii. 15.
[2] Ezek. xx. 28 (see *v.* 29); 1 Kings iii. 2; xxii. 43, &c.

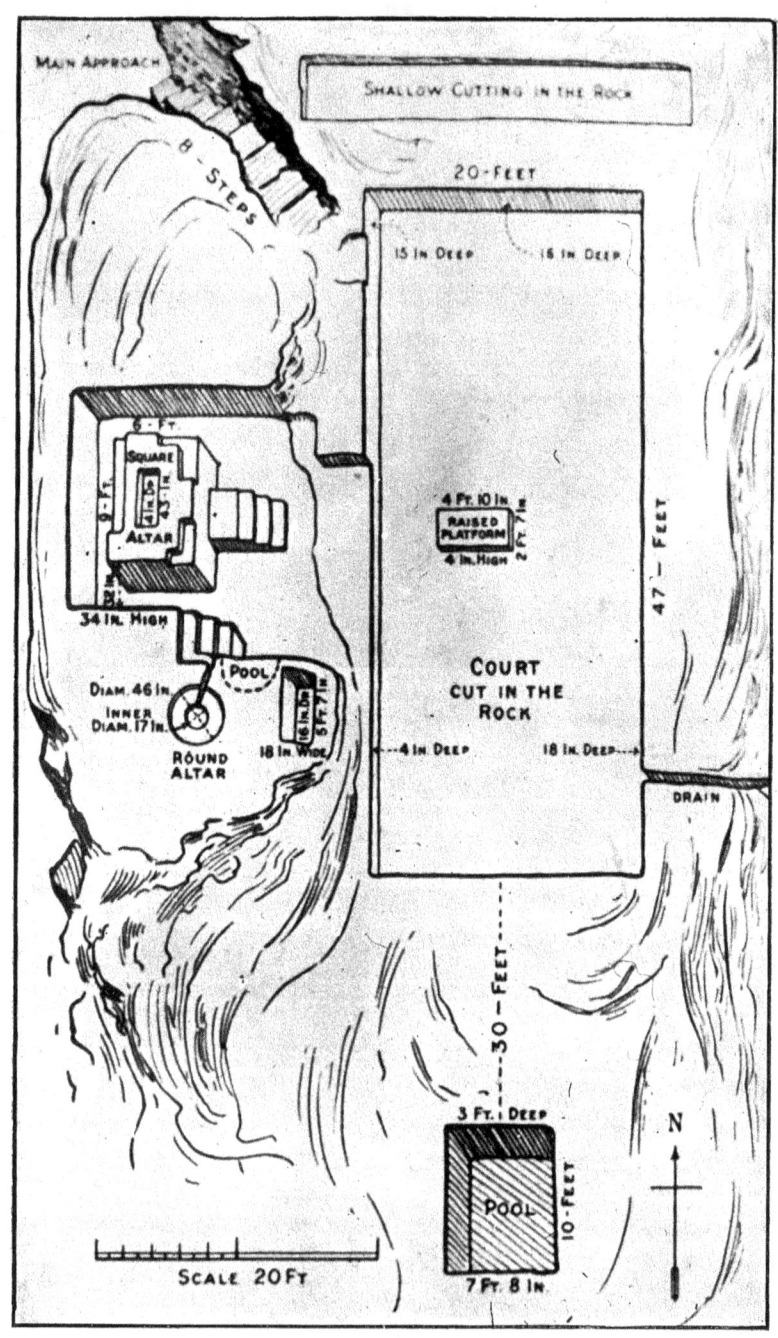

PLAN OF ROCK-CUT HIGH PLACE ABOVE PETRA

From Nielsen, *Die altarabische Mondreligion und die Mosaïsche Ueberlieferung* (1904), p. 176 (also in the *Biblical World*, January, 1901, Frontispiece).

also, at least in some cases, with buildings for the sacred meals, like the one of which Samuel and Saul partook, and for the priests to live in,[1] and shrines for the images:[2] but little more was known about them.

Within the last few years, however, several such high places have been discovered. The first to be discovered[3] was not in Palestine, but on the hills above Petra, the romantically situated capital of the ancient Edom.[4] Petra lies in an amphitheatre of red sandstone rocks, the sides of which, rising almost perpendicularly from the plain, are high up simply honeycombed with caves, used anciently, some as dwellings, others as tombs. It is accessible, practically, only from the east, through the narrow gorge called the Sik, about $1\frac{1}{2}$ miles long, at some parts hardly more than 12 feet wide, and bounded symmetrically on both sides by perpendicular sandstone rocks of exquisite colouring, from one to two hundred feet high.[5] As the traveller enters the amphitheatre from the Sik, he sees facing him the so-called 'Pharaoh's Treasury.'[6]; a little further on, he sees on the left an immense theatre, with thirty-three tiers of seats, and then many other ruins of ancient buildings, and high up on both sides the dwellings and tombs hewn out of the rock.[7] A little to the left of Pharaoh's Treasury, a narrow path leads up picturesquely, through a tangle of trees and bushes, and fantastically shaped, iris-coloured rocks, to the top of the hills, south-east of the theatre, on which the high place is. Here, on a large level ledge of rock, some 500 ft. long by 100 ft. broad, we see first a rectangular area, or court, 47 ft. long from north to south, and 20 ft. from east to

---

[1] Notice the expression, 'house of high places' (1 Kings xii. 31; xiii. 32; 2 Kings xvii. 29, 32; xxiii. 19); and the verbs 'build' (1 Kings xiv. 23; 2 Kings xvii. 9; xxi. 3; Jer. vii. 31; xix. 5; xxxii. 35) and 'break down' (2 Kings xxiii. 8, 15), used in connexion with 'high places'. In 2 Kings xxiii. 15 read with LXX,' and brake in pieces its stones' for ' and *burned* the high place'.

[2] 2 Kings xvii. 29.

[3] See G. L. Robinson in the *Biblical World* (Chicago), Jan. 1901, pp. 6-16 (with photographs); S. Ives Curtiss, *QS*. 00. 350-5; and especially the account that has appeared since these lectures were delivered in G. Dalman's elaborate and finely illustrated work, *Petra und seine Felsheiligtümer* (1908), p. 157 ff.

[4] See particulars about Petra, with many photographs, in Libbey and Hoskins, *The Jordan Valley and Petra* (1905), vol. ii.

[5] See the illustrations in Libbey and Hoskins, pp. 71, 73, 76.

[6] See the illustrations in Libbey and Hoskins, pp. 79, 83.

[7] Cf. the allusion to these rock-dwellings in Obad. 3 ' O thou that dwellest in the retreats of the rocks, the height of (LXX "that maketh high") his dwelling, that saith in his heart, "Who will bring me down to the ground?"' The verse reappears in substantially the same form in Jer. xlix. 16.

west, cut out of the rock: about 15 ft. to the west of this court, with four steps leading up to it, there is a large altar, also cut out of the rock, 9 ft. long, 6 ft. wide, and 3 ft. high, with a rectangular hollow on the top, perhaps intended for the fire. Nearly in front of the altar, towards the middle of the large court, is a small raised platform of rock, 4 in. high, and 4 ft. 10 in. from west to east, and 2 ft. 7 in. from north to south. The court, which is approached by steps leading up into it at its north-west corner, was, it may be supposed, the place set apart for the worshippers in front of the altar; the raised platform facing the altar may have served as a table at which the worshippers partook of the sacred meal (Guthe), or on which unbloody offerings were presented to the deity, according to a custom prevalent at other sanctuaries (Dalman). The altar is separated from the adjoining rock, out of which it was cut, on the north, west, and south, by a passage-way, about 3 ft. wide, with steps at its southeast corner leading down into it from the surface of the rock. South of this passage-way, on the south side of the altar, is a rock platform, 11 ft. 9 in. from north to south, and 16 ft. 6 in. from east to west, with a circular depression cut into it 3 ft. 10 in. in diameter, intended, perhaps, for libations (so Dalman).[1] A little east of this is a large rock-cut trough, at which presumably ablutions were performed. Some 30 ft. south of the court is a large cistern, which has been excavated in the rock, used probably as a reservoir of water. Whether the two large monoliths, about 100 ft. apart, cut out of the rock, at a little distance from the court, had a sacred character, as the first explorers supposed, is doubtful.[2] The sacred place does not seem to be of more ancient date than shortly before the Christian era.[3]

The high place at Gezer[4] was on the east declivity of the western hill. The temple-area, or court for the worshippers, is not indicated as it is at Petra, nor are there remains of any altar: but the superb series of eight huge monoliths, standing in a row, leaves little doubt as to what the place was. The eight stones were originally ten: for the stumps of two that have been broken still remain at the north end. These stones are evidently the *mazzēbāhs*, or 'standing-stones', —A.V. 'pillars', sometimes wrongly 'images', R.V. always 'pillars'— of the Old Testament. The *mazzēbāh*—originally, it is probable,

[1] Against Robinson's view (indicated in the Plan) that this may have been a second altar, see Guthe, *Mitteilungen und Nachrichten des Deutschen Palästina-Vereins*, 1905, p. 50 f.
[2] Dalman, p. 181 f. (where also there are photographs of the monoliths).
[3] This, though the most finished, is not the only high place at Petra; there are several others, which are described and illustrated by Dalman.
[4] *QS.* 03. 23–32.

COURT OF THE HIGH PLACE ABOVE PETRA
The altar is in the recess at the centre of the left-hand side of the court.
From Nielsen, op. cit., p. 172.

THE ALTAR OF THE HIGH PLACE ABOVE PETRA
From Nielsen, op. cit., p. 175.

[*By permission of the Palestine Exploration Fund.*

ROW OF STANDING-STONES AT GEZER

From the *Quarterly Statement*, 1903, p. 26.

To face p. 63]

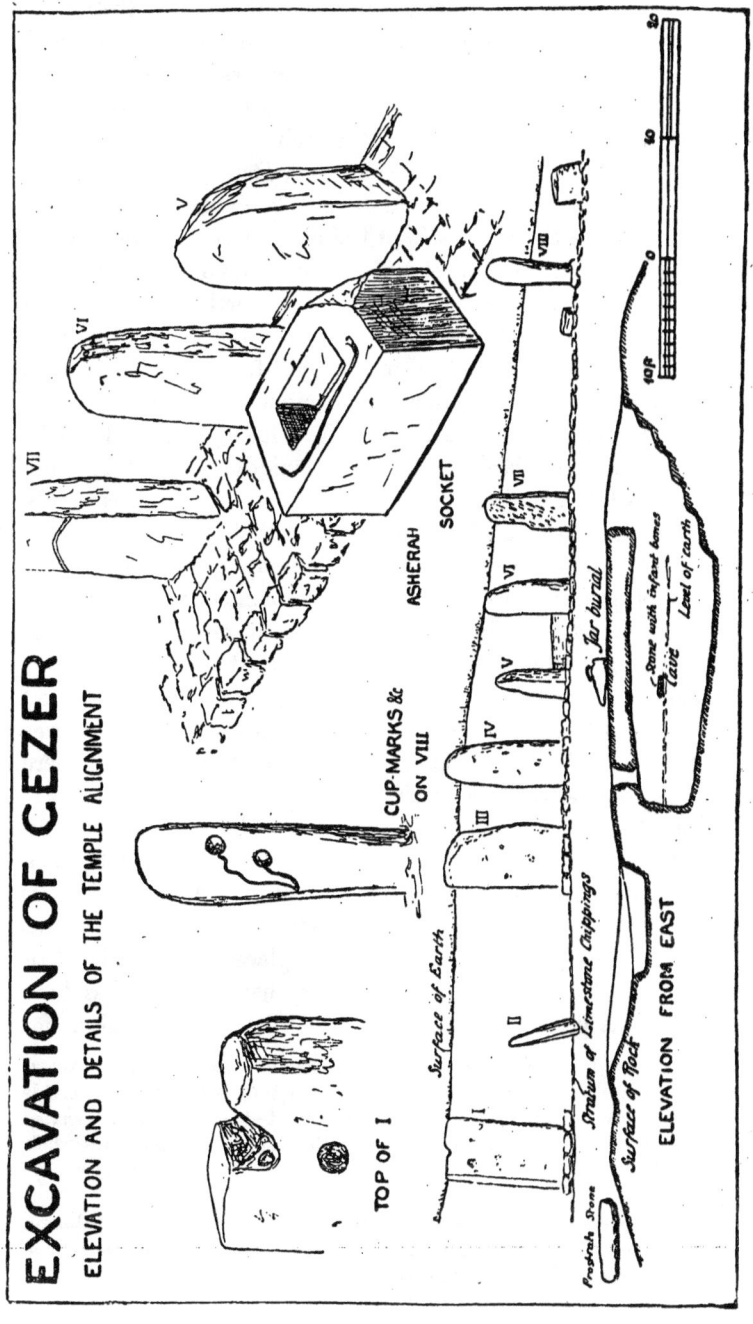

Elevation and Details of the Standing-stones at Gezer

conceived as the abode of a deity—appears in the Old Testament as the distinguishing mark of a holy place, and as often erected beside an altar, especially in Canaanite sanctuaries (Exod. xxiii. 24; Deut. vii. 5; xii. 2, 3; 2 Kings x. 26 f.; cf., as set up by Israelites, 1 Kings xiv. 23; 2 Kings xvii. 10).[1] The Israelites were commanded to destroy the Canaanite standing-stones (Exod., Deut. *ll. cc.*), and were forbidden to erect such stones beside Jehovah's altar (Deut. xvi. 22). Here, then, we have the *mazzēbāhs* of the high place of Gezer. They are just large unhewn blocks, set on end, and supported at the base by smaller stones. They stand in a line due north and south, and range in height from 10 ft. 6 in. to 5 ft. 5 in.: the largest of them, the first on the south, is 4 ft. 7 in. broad, by 2 ft. 6 in. thick, so that it takes four persons clasping hands to encircle it. In front of the fifth monolith there is a stone block 2 ft. 6 in. high, 6 ft. by 5 ft. along the sides, with a large cavity in the middle, nearly 3 ft. long, 2 ft. broad, and 1 ft. 4 in. deep. The use of this cavity is not certainly known: Mr. Macalister at first[2] conjectured that it was a socket to hold an 'Ashérah'—the wooden post, representing, as it seems, the sacred tree, often mentioned in the Old Testament in connexion with an altar or *mazzēbāh*[3]—for which, however, it seems to be larger than is probable; afterwards he thought that it might be a laver for ceremonial ablutions:[4] later still, in 1907, he expressed himself as very uncertain about it.[5] Père Vincent thinks that it was simply an altar. Professor Kittel[6] regards it as the place where the animals to be offered were slaughtered.

Just on the east of the northernmost of the monoliths is an entrance leading down into two large caves, connected with each other by a narrow passage.[7] These caves were at one time residences of the cave-dwellers; when discovered, however, the smaller cave was found to have been closed by large blocks placed against the door inside, so that it was turned into a secret chamber. It has been conjectured that it was used, in connexion with the high place, for

---

[1] *Mazzēbāhs* are not anywhere in the Old Testament described expressly as standing by high places; but the manner in which they are mentioned beside them (1 Kings xiv. 23; 2 Kings xviii. 4; cf. xvii. 9-11), and also associated closely with Canaanite sanctuaries, leaves little doubt that that was their regular position.

[2] *QS.* 03. 31.

[3] See, e.g., in the Revised Version, Exod. xxxiv. 13; Deut. xvi. 21; Judges vi. 25, 26; 1 Kings xiv. 23, xvi. 33; 2 Kings xvii. 10. In the Authorized Version the word is incorrectly translated 'grove'.

[4] *Bible Side-Lights from the Mound of Gezer* (1906), p. 66.

[5] Kittel, *Studien zur hebr. Archäologie* (1908), p. 132.   [6] Ibid.

[7] *QS.* 03. 24 f.

Standing-stones in a Temple at Megiddo
From *Tell el-Mutesellim*, p. 110 (Fig. 167).

[To face p. 65]

STANDING-STONES FOUND IN CANAAN

the purpose of giving oracles; the inquirer went into the outer chamber, and a priest stationed in the inner chamber answered his questions.

A second high place, with a row of four standing-stones, and the stump of a fifth, dating from about 1400 B.C., was found at Gezer in 1905.[1]

There have also been found several *maẓẓēbāhs* at Taanach,[2] including a double row of five; and at Tell el-Mutesellim, in excavating a temple, a large room or court was found containing two.[3] In some of these *maẓẓēbāhs* holes had been cut, sometimes at the top, in other cases at the sides; these, it has been supposed, were for the purpose of receiving libations, whether of blood or (Gen. xxviii. 18) oil, offered to the *numen* supposed to reside in the stone.[4] The belief that a stone was the abode of a *numen* or deity was, and still is, widely diffused among primitive and semi-primitive peoples:[5] Is. lvii. 6 speaks of libations poured out by idolatrous Israelites to the 'smooth stones of the valley'; and the act of Jacob in anointing with oil the stone which he had used as his pillow (Gen. xxviii. 18), clearly stands in some relation to the same belief.[6]

It seems indeed that there are still remains of ancient high places in Palestine even on the surface of the soil. Many years ago, Architect Schick, who during his long residence in Jerusalem had closely studied the archaeology of the country, had observed near Zar‘a (the Zor‘ah of Samson, Judges xiii. 25), fifteen miles west of Jerusalem, a large quadrangular surface of rock, with a number of cup-shaped depressions in it, and with steps leading up to it, and platforms around it, which had every appearance of being an ancient rock-altar, and also another smaller construction of the same kind near Marmīta[7]; and Guthe, in 1891,[8] called attention to other similar constructions, which had been noticed elsewhere.[9] More recently

---

[1] *QS*. 07. 267 f.

[2] *Tell Ta'annek*, pp. 18, 69, 72. See below, p. 84.

[3] For *maẓẓēbāhs* in a Temple cf. 2 Kings x. 26.

[4] Kittel, op. cit., pp. 127-31.

[5] See the note in the writer's *Book of Genesis*, p. 267, with the references.

[6] It is noticeable that in ver. 22 it is not the place, but the *stone*, which Jacob says is to be 'God's house', or abode.

[7] *Zeitschrift des Deutschen Palästina-Vereins*, x. (1887), p. 140 ff. See Kittel, *Studien zur hebr. Archäologie*, pp. 105-8, 120-2, where the illustrations are taken from Plates III and IV at the end of Schick's article. Marmīta is about 2 miles S.E. of Zar‘a.

[8] *Z. des Deutschen Pal.-Vereins*, xiii. (1890), p. 123 ff. Rocks with cup-marks were found also at Tell eṣ-Ṣāfi and Tell Sandaḥannah (Vincent, p. 95).

[9] In the same article, Guthe also called attention to the dolmens or other

66 CANAAN AS KNOWN THROUGH EXCAVATION

Professor Kittel[1] has found nearly at the top of the hills of Neby Samwil and el-Jib—almost certainly the sites of the ancient Mizpah and Gibeon—level surfaces of rock, with cup-shaped depressions

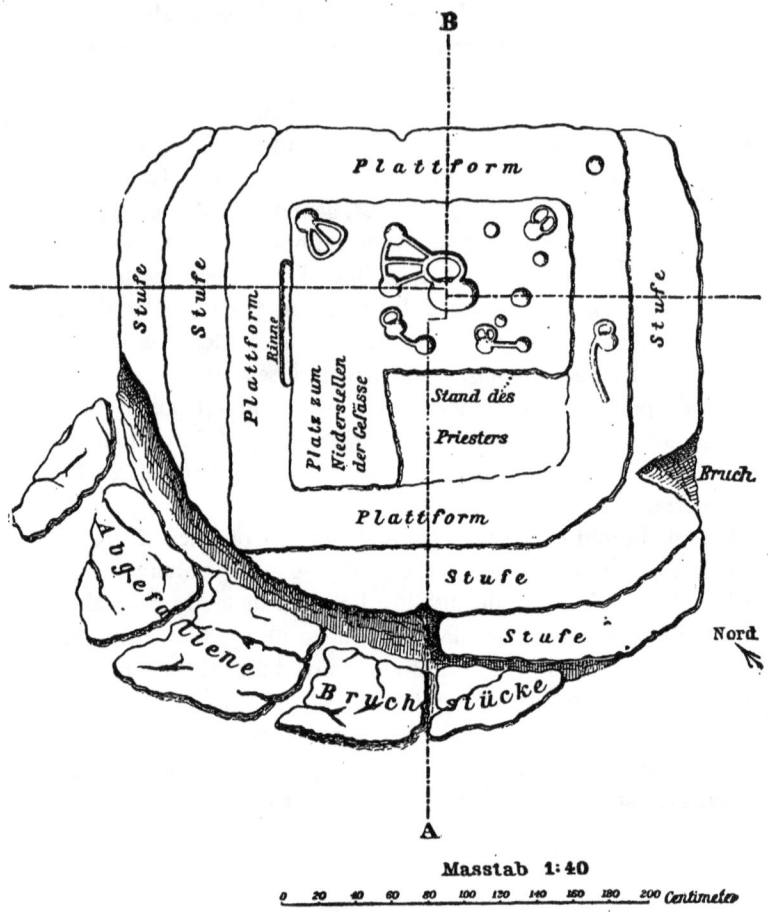

THE ROCK-ALTAR AT ZAR'A

From Kittel's *Studien zur hebräischen Archäologie und Religionsgeschichte* (1908), p. 105.

hollowed out in them, similar to those found at Gezer, which bear every evidence of having been anciently high places: at Mizpah,

large stones, with cup-shaped hollows in them, which had been noticed in different parts of Palestine, especially on the east of Jordan, and which presumably had been once used for the reception of libations. Several of these had been noted by Conder in the *Survey of Eastern Palestine*, 1889 (e. g. pp. 20, 23, 24, 268 [one with forty holes], 270); cf. his *Heth and Moab*, chap. viii.

[1] *Studien, &c.* pp. 137, 140.

THE NORTHERN BLOCK OF THE ROCK-ALTAR AT MEGIDDO
From *Tell el-Mutesellim*, p. 156.

[*By permission of the Palestine Exploration Fund.*
SACRIFICED INFANT BURIED IN A JAR
From *Bible Side-Lights from the Mound of Gezer*, p. 72 (Vincent, p. 190).

it is said (1 Sam. vii. 6), water was poured out 'before Jehovah' by the Israelites assembled there to meet Samuel; and the rock-surface at el-Jib may be the actual 'great high place' where the Gibeonites hung up 'before Jehovah' the seven grandsons of Saul

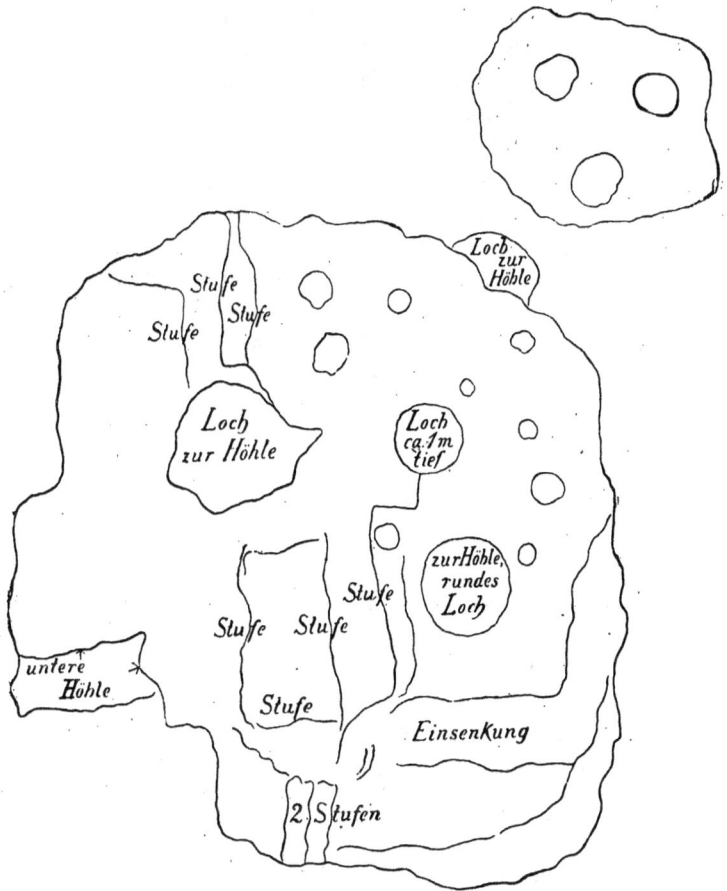

ROCK-SURFACE AT MEGIDDO, WITH CUP-SHAPED DEPRESSIONS, AND A CAVE UNDERNEATH

From Kittel, op. cit., p. 143.

(2 Sam. xxi. 6, 8 f.), and at which Solomon offered 1,000 burnt offerings, and where he had his famous dream (1 Kings iii. 4, 5 ff.). And at Megiddo Dr. Schumacher has found a large level surface of rock with similar cup-shaped depressions, and also with holes forming entrances to a subterranean cave, which remind us of the caves found under the similar rock-surface at Gezer (above, p. 51).

In the stratum of earth underlying the high place at Gezer a very noteworthy discovery was made;[1] it was found, viz., to contain a cemetery of infants, deposited in large earthenware jars. The infants were all newly born, probably not more than a week old. A cemetery containing some twenty infants, buried also in jars, about a rock-altar, was found afterwards at Taanach.[2] This was of earlier date than the one found at Gezer; it was not in proximity to any row of monoliths; and the ages of the infants were in several cases as much as five years. At Megiddo there were found buried beneath a corner of the temple just mentioned, containing the standing-stones, four jars with bones, very like those found at Gezer, belonging, as was shown by the slight depth at which they were found, and by their style, to the late Israelite period.[3] Usually there were also deposited, either inside the jar, or outside near it, two or three smaller vessels, generally a bowl and a jug—intended, no doubt, to supply the food, which, in accordance with ancient belief, the infant might need in the other world.

It is commonly supposed that these bones are those of infants—in all probability, firstborn—sacrificed, in accordance with a widely prevalent Semitic custom, to some deity. Père Vincent (p. 194 f.) only doubts this in the case of the Taanach infants, agreeing with what had been first supposed by Professor Sellin[4], that these may have been children who had died too young to be buried in the family sepulchres. We know from Greek writers that the Phoenicians and Carthaginians, in times of grave national danger or calamity, were in the habit of sacrificing children for the purpose of either appeasing the anger, or obtaining the help, of the national deity. In the second book of Kings (iii. 27) we read that Mesha, king of Moab, when hard pressed by the invading Israelites, sacrificed his eldest son to Chemosh, the national god of Moab. The practice found its way into Judah under the later kings, especially Ahaz and Manasseh, and is often alluded to by the prophets of the seventh century B.C. Thus Micah, in a well-known passage (vi. 7), represents an Israelite as asking—

> Shall I give my firstborn for my transgression?
> The fruit of my body for the sin of my soul?

But more than this, it was also the custom to regard the firstborn of men, not less than the firstborn of animals, and the firstfruits of the field, as sacred to the national deity. And the principle was recognized in Hebrew law, though in Israel its application was

---

[1] *QS.* 03. 32-4.
[2] Sellin, *Tell Ta'annek*, pp. 35-8.
[3] See the Plate opposite.
[4] *Tell Ta'annek*, p. 36.

JARS CONTAINING THE BONES OF INFANTS FOUND NEAR THE CORNER
OF A TEMPLE AT MEGIDDO

From *Tell el-Mutesellim* (Fig. 181), p. 121 (see p. 122).

[*By permission of the Palestine Exploration Fund.*

JUGS DEPOSITED IN THE GRAVES OF INFANTS AT GEZER

Cf. Vincent, p. 189.

JAR-BURIED INFANTS 69

rendered harmless by the firstborn of men being redeemed at a money valuation, only the firstborn of clean animals, such as the ox and the sheep, being actually offered in sacrifice to Jehovah.[1] If the explanation be correct, we should have ocular evidence of this gruesome practice, as it was carried out by the primitive Semitic inhabitants of Palestine, and even, at least at Megiddo, in the Israelite period.[2]

The *fifth* and *sixth* strata represent the earlier and later periods of the occupation of Canaan by the Israelites.[3] Iron now begins to appear, though bronze is still the ordinary metal. In the fifth stratum private houses are found to have encroached upon the precincts of the high place. Mr. Macalister[4] attributes this encroachment to the fact that at the Hebrew occupation the population of Gezer was increased by Israelites as well as Canaanites crowding within its walls. After the fifth stratum, also, the eastern hill is deserted, and the city thus reduced to two-thirds of its former size; and this Mr. Macalister would explain by supposing that when Pharaoh burnt the city, and slew the Canaanite population, Solomon, when he rebuilt it, would have only the smaller Israelite population to provide for. Both these explanations, however, appear to rest upon an incorrect exegesis of Joshua xvi. 10 ('They drave not out the Canaanites that dwelt in Gezer; but the Canaanites dwelt in the midst of Ephraim unto this day, and became servants to do forced labour'), which states not that Israelites and Canaanites dwelt together in Gezer, but simply that the Canaanites maintained themselves in Gezer in the midst of an Israelite population outside.

In the fifth stratum six or eight instances were found in which the bones of infants had been built under or into ordinary house walls.[5] Inside one of the buildings, dating from the latter half of the Jewish monarchy, in whose walls one of these skeletons was found, were also two skeletons of infants contained in jars—the latest examples of

---

[1] Exod. xiii. 12-13.

[2] In the absence of inscriptions, speaking distinctly, the explanation remains of course a conjecture; and, this being so, the suggestion of Prof. J. G. Frazer in *Adonis, Attis, and Osiris*, ed. 2 (1907), p. 82 f., may deserve consideration. It is believed viz. among many primitive peoples (ibid. pp. 77 ff.)—in India and Australia, for instance—that the souls of the dead may be re-born; and where this belief prevails infants are often buried under a threshold or near a house, in order that their souls may be re-born into the family: Mr. Frazer accordingly suggests that these skeletons are those of infants who had died a natural death, and had been buried by their parents under a sanctuary in the hope that, quickened by a divine power, they might again, as their own mother's children, be born into the world. (I am indebted for this reference to Mr. S. A. Cook.)

[3] *QS*. 03. 13; cf. 287-9.

[4] *QS*. 03. 11, 32, 49 f.

[5] *QS*. 03. 224.

70 CANAAN AS KNOWN THROUGH EXCAVATION

this form of sepulture at present known. Afterwards, the skeleton of an *adult*, a woman of advanced age, lying on its side—with a bowl by the head, and a large two-handled jar between the thighs and legs, probably intended as food-vessels—was found deposited in a hollow under the corner of a house: in another house also were found two infants buried in jars at the corners of rooms, and an adult lying in the middle of a chamber.[1] Elsewhere, under the corner of a wall was found the head of a little girl, about 2½ years old.[2] Since this lecture was delivered, also, there have been found under the foundations of a building belonging to an earlier period,

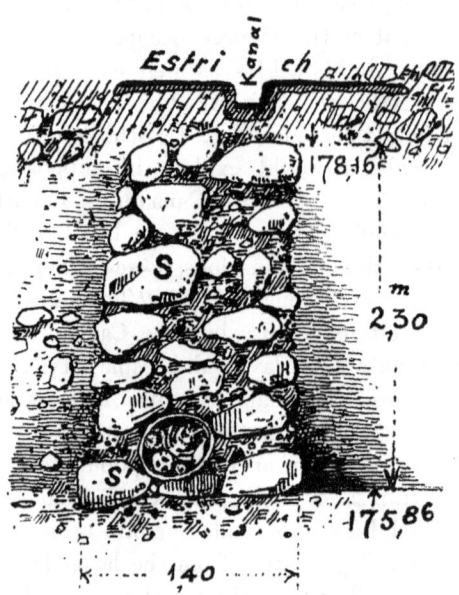

JAR CONTAINING THE BONES OF AN INFANT AT THE BOTTOM OF
A WALL AT MEGIDDO

From *Tell el-Mutesellim*, p. 45 (Fig. 41).

the XIIth Egyptian Dynasty (*c.* 2000 B.C.), the skeletons of two men, laid out at length, with bowls and jugs beside them, and with the hand of one of the skeletons in one of the bowls, as if helping himself out of it.[3] At Megiddo the skeleton of a girl, about fifteen years old, was found built in at the base of a large fortified tower.[4] And at Taanach Professor Sellin discovered, exactly at the foot of the tower protecting the main entrance to the west fort, the skeleton of

---

[1] *QS.* 05. 198 f.   [2] *QS.* 07. 268.   [3] *QS.* 08. 206 f. (with illustration).
[4] *Tell el-Mutesellim*, p. 54; Vincent, p. 50 f., 197 (with illustration).

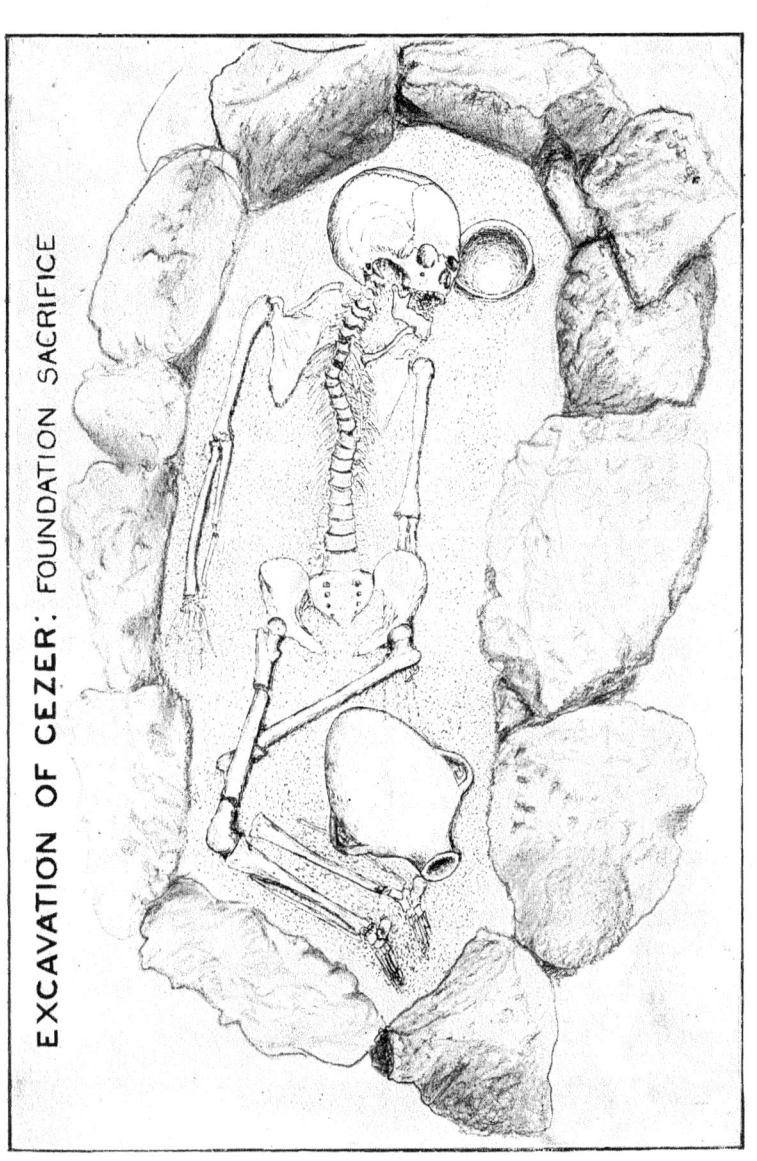

Skeleton of a Woman found in a Hollow under the Corner of a House at Gezer
From the *Quarterly Statement*, 1904, p. 17.

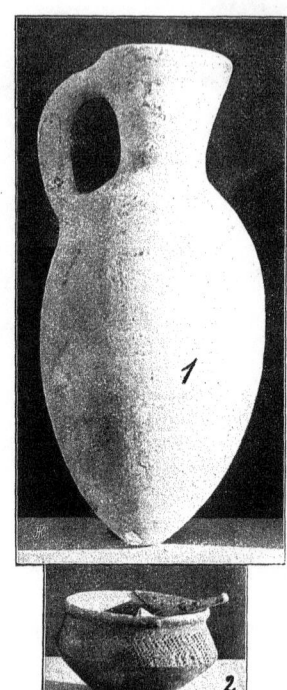

VESSELS FROM THE JAR CONTAINING AN INFANT'S BONES FOUND AT MEGIDDO (see p. 70).

From *Tell el-Mutesellim*, p. 46 (Fig. 42).

a child about ten years old, with two jars, a large and a small one, and a clay bowl, supported on a foot, all of particularly fine workmanship.[1]

It can scarcely be doubted that these are examples of foundation-sacrifices, i. e. of sacrifices offered at the foundation of a building, for the purpose of ensuring the stability of the structure and the welfare of those about to occupy or use it. Traces of this custom are to be found in the legends or practices of people in the most different parts of the world, not only, for instance, in India, New Zealand, China, Japan, and Mexico, but also in Germany, Denmark, and our own country. Numerous examples have been collected by Dr. Tylor in his *Primitive Culture* (i. 94-7), by Dr. Trumbull in his *Threshold Covenant* (1890), pp. 45-57, and in an article on 'Kirkgrims', i. e. apparitions of animals supposed to have been buried under the foundations of a church, in the *Cornhill Magazine* for February, 1887 (cited by Trumbull).[2] Thus there are many stories and legends of workmen being unable to complete a building—a church, castle, bridge, &c.—without the sacrifice of a human being; and so a child, the wife of the chief mason, a slave, a criminal, as the case might be, was immured, sometimes alive, for the purpose. At Scutari, for instance, it is said that the workmen could not make the fortifications stand, till they seized a girl who brought them their dinner, and immured her. According to a Scottish legend, St. Columba was unable to build a cathedral on the island of Iona, till he could secure its stability by a human sacrifice; so he took his companion, Oran, and buried him alive in the foundations, after which he had no further trouble. In Alaska, till in 1867 it came into the possession of the United States, human sacrifices were common at the foundation of a new house; a slave was blindfolded, and laid down under the place selected for the fireplace and throttled, and four other slaves were also made to stand in the holes for the four corner-posts and barbarously felled to the ground with a club.[3] When the Bridge Gate of the city walls of Bremen was demolished a few years ago, it is said that the skeleton of a child was found imbedded in the foundations. Naturally in many places an animal has taken the place of the original human victim. So, for instance, when the ground was broken for the railway from Beirut to Damascus, ten sheep were placed in a row on the ground, and their throats were cut; and when the foundations of a government school were laid at

---

[1] *Tell Ta'annek*, p. 51; Vincent, p. 200.
[2] Cf. S. Ives Curtiss, *Primitive Semitic Religion To-day* (1902), p. 184.
[3] Trumbull, op. cit., p. 51, in an extract from W. G. Chase's 'Notes from Alaska' in the *Journal of American Folk-Lore*, vi. 51.

Kerak, two sheep were slaughtered. In Greece when the foundations of a new house are being laid, a fowl or lamb is killed, and its blood smeared on the foundation-stone: if this ceremony be omitted, the first person entering the house is supposed to be liable to die. That more examples have not been found in Palestine seems to show that such sacrifices were not offered regularly, but only on important or exceptional occasions.

There has been supposed to be one case of such a foundation-sacrifice recorded in the Old Testament, on the occasion viz. of the rebuilding of Jericho; but it is doubtful whether the supposition is correct. Joshua, it will be remembered, after Jericho had been entered and burnt by the Israelites, is said to have uttered a curse upon any one who should essay to rebuild it, 'with the loss of his firstborn shall he lay the foundation thereof, and with the loss of his youngest son shall he set up the gates thereof' (Joshua vi. 26). The curse is said to have fallen upon Hiel the Bethelite, who in the days of Ahab 'laid the foundation thereof with the loss of Abiram his firstborn, and set up the gates thereof with the loss of his youngest son Segub' (1 Kings xvi. 34). This is commonly explained to mean that Hiel lost his sons through some accident happening to them while the work of rebuilding was in progress. And there certainly are difficulties in the supposition that a foundation-sacrifice is referred to. The curse implies that something unusual and unexpected would happen to Hiel. But if a foundation-sacrifice was a custom of the time, there would be nothing unusual about it,—unless, indeed, it might be supposed that there was something exceptional in the circumstances of Hiel's case, as if, instead of some slave or prisoner being taken as the victim, Hiel's sons were made the victims by some cause beyond their father's control, being drawn, for instance, by lot, or chosen in some way by the people against their father's wish. As such a supposition, however, is not required, or even suggested, by the text, and is, indeed, purely hypothetical, it must remain uncertain whether foundation-sacrifices are really alluded to in connexion with the rebuilding of Jericho.

In one case,[1] by the side of a large jar containing the bones of two infants, there were found two bowls, two saucers, two jugs, and also two lamps; there was also found frequently, first in City IV at Tell el-Ḥesy,[2] and afterwards at Gezer in the fifth and sixth strata,[3] and also elsewhere,[4] near the foundations of walls, but unaccompanied

---

[1] *QS.* 03. 307. The deposit belonged to an early Canaanite stratum.
[2] Bliss, *A Mound of Many Cities*, p. 84.   [3] *QS.* 03. 205 f. ; cf. 03. 8, 10.
[4] As at Tell Zakariya, 2½ ft. below the foundations of rude walls (*QS.* 99. 183).

[*By permission of the Palestine Exploration Fund.*

NORMAL LAMP AND BOWL GROUP

From the *Quarterly Statement*, 1903, p. 205.

by any infants in jars, a lamp, buried between two bowls, one above and one below, i.e., it would seem, the lamp between the two bowls took the place of the sacrificed infant in a jar. It is supposed by Mr. Macalister that the lamp and bowl was at first intended as a symbol of the act of sacrifice, the lamp symbolizing the fire, and the bowl containing blood or some substitute for it; but that in course of time, as religious ideas became higher, and the inhumanity of child-sacrifices was realized, the human victim was omitted, and only the symbols—the lamp and bowl—were retained. These symbolical deposits—if this is the right explanation of them— begin as early as the fifteenth century B.C., in the Canaanite period [1]; but they seem never to have entirely superseded the human sacrifice, for cases of these occur at a date not much later than that of Solomon, and the two instances mentioned above (p. 69) of infants found buried in jars are referred to the latter half of the Jewish monarchy.[2]

On the east of the Troglodyte high place there were found in 1905 two graves, and in 1907 two more, all of a kind different from any that had been met with before.[3] They were built of masonry, not hollowed out as caves in the rock; the bodies were laid out in them at full length, not in a contracted position; pottery was practically absent, whereas in the Semitic tombs it was abundant; the bodies were decked in ornament, of which in the other tombs there was no trace; the deposits were of artistic value, consisting, for instance, of gold, silver, and alabaster, which in the Semitic tombs were either absent altogether or meagre. Mr. Macalister suggested provisionally that these, so different from all others found at Gezer, might be Philistine tombs. Mr. (now Professor) J. L. Myres,[4] after examining the artistic objects found in them, declared that they recalled the art of Cyprus in the period next following the Mycenaean age; and he considers that the tombs are those of a people who had invaded the Philistine coastland in the period of the Sea Raids, and maintained themselves there, in occasional contact with Cyprus, but not with anything further west, for a century or two after the tenth. The Philistines are probably the *Purasati* of the Egyptian inscriptions—a plundering people who, coming from the south-west coasts of Asia Minor and the Aegean isles in the reign of Rameses III (*c.* 1200 B.C.), swept down upon the south-west of Canaan and secured a footing there. 'To call them,' says Mr. Myres, 'the tombs of "Aegean Intruders" would, I think, be safe already; to label them provisionally "Philistine" would not be over-bold.' When the sites of some of the

---

[1] *QS*. 03. 8 f.; Vincent, p. 198 f.
[2] *QS*. 03. 224.
[3] *QS*. 05. 318-22; 07. 185, 197 ff.
[4] *QS*. 07. 240-3.

ancient Philistine cities have been excavated, we may be able to speak more definitely about these interesting tombs.

At Tell eṣ-Ṣâfi, and the three other places—Tell Zakariya, Tell Sandaḥannah, and Tell ej-Judeideh—excavated by Dr. Bliss and Mr. Macalister in 1898–1900, there were found a number of stamped jar-handles of considerable interest. Twenty-five of these were stamped with names, altogether eight in number—such as Shebaniah, [son of] 'Azariah, 'Azzur, [son of] Haggai, Menahem, [son of] Shebaniah—evidently either of the potter who made the vessels, or of their owner.[1] In addition to these there were, not counting twenty-seven on which the names were illegible, fifty-three of a different type,[2] with the device of a winged scarabaeus impressed upon them, and bearing the names of four towns—Hebron, Ziph,[3] Socoh,[4] and Mamshith,[5] preceded by a word which, according to the vowels supplied to the unvocalized Hebrew, would yield, as the rendering of the legend as a whole, either, 'Of the king of Hebron, of Ziph,' &c., or, 'Of (*or* For) the king. Hebron,' 'Of (*or* For) the king. Ziph,' &c.[6] At first it was thought that the first of these renderings might be adopted, in which case the stamps would be very interesting memorials of the age before the Israelitish conquest, when, as we learn from the traditions preserved in the Book of Joshua, Palestine

[1] Bliss and Macalister, *Excavations in Palestine*, pp. 119 ff.; or *QS*. 05. 323. See on the opposite page Nos. 20–23, 28.

[2] *Excavations in Palestine*, pp. 106 ff.; or *QS*. 99. 104–6, 184–6. See Nos. 1–10, 12–14, 16–17, opposite.

NOTES ON THE PLATE OPPOSITE. 1–3. 'Of the king. Hebron.' 4–9. 'Of the king. Socoh.' 10, 12, 13, 14. 'Of the King. Ziph.' 16, 17. 'Of the king. Mamshith.' 20. הושע צפן 'Hoshea, [son of] Zaphan. 21. [ע]זריהו שבניהו 'Shebaniah, [son of] 'Azariah.' 22. לנחם עברי 'Of Naḥam, [son of] 'Abdi.' 23. שבניה עזריה 'Shebaniah, [son of] 'Azariah.' 28. לעזר חגי 'Of 'Azzur, [son of] Haggai' [or '*Ezer*: we cannot be sure of the vowels]. The stamps marked J were found at Tell ej-Judeideh; the one marked Z is from Tell Zakariya.

[3] Joshua xv. 55; 1 Sam. xxiii. 14 *al.*, now *Tell Zif*, 4 miles south of Hebron.

[4] Either the Socoh of Joshua xv. 35 (in the 'lowland'), 1 Sam. xvii. 1, now probably *esh-Shuweikeh*, 16 miles south-south-west of Jerusalem, 13 miles north-west of Hebron, and 5 miles north-east of Tell ej-Judeideh; or the Socoh of Joshua xv. 48 (in the 'hill country' of Judah), now *esh-Shuweikeh*, 10 miles south-west of Hebron.

[5] Probably (Hommel, *Expos. Times*, March, 1901, p. 288, cf. April, p. 336) the *Mapsis* of Eusebius, *Onom.* (ed. Lagarde) 210. 86, and the *Mampsis* of Jerome, *Onom.* 85. 3, a day's journey (= about 20 miles) south of Hebron.

[6] Six, with (as far as could be read) the same names, were also found by Sir C. Warren deep down at the south-east angle of the Ḥaram area at Jerusalem (*Recovery of Jerusalem*, p. 474 f.). Several have also been found at Gezer, including one with the name 'Mamshith', but without 'Of the king' (*QS*. 08. 281).

STAMPED JAR-HANDLES

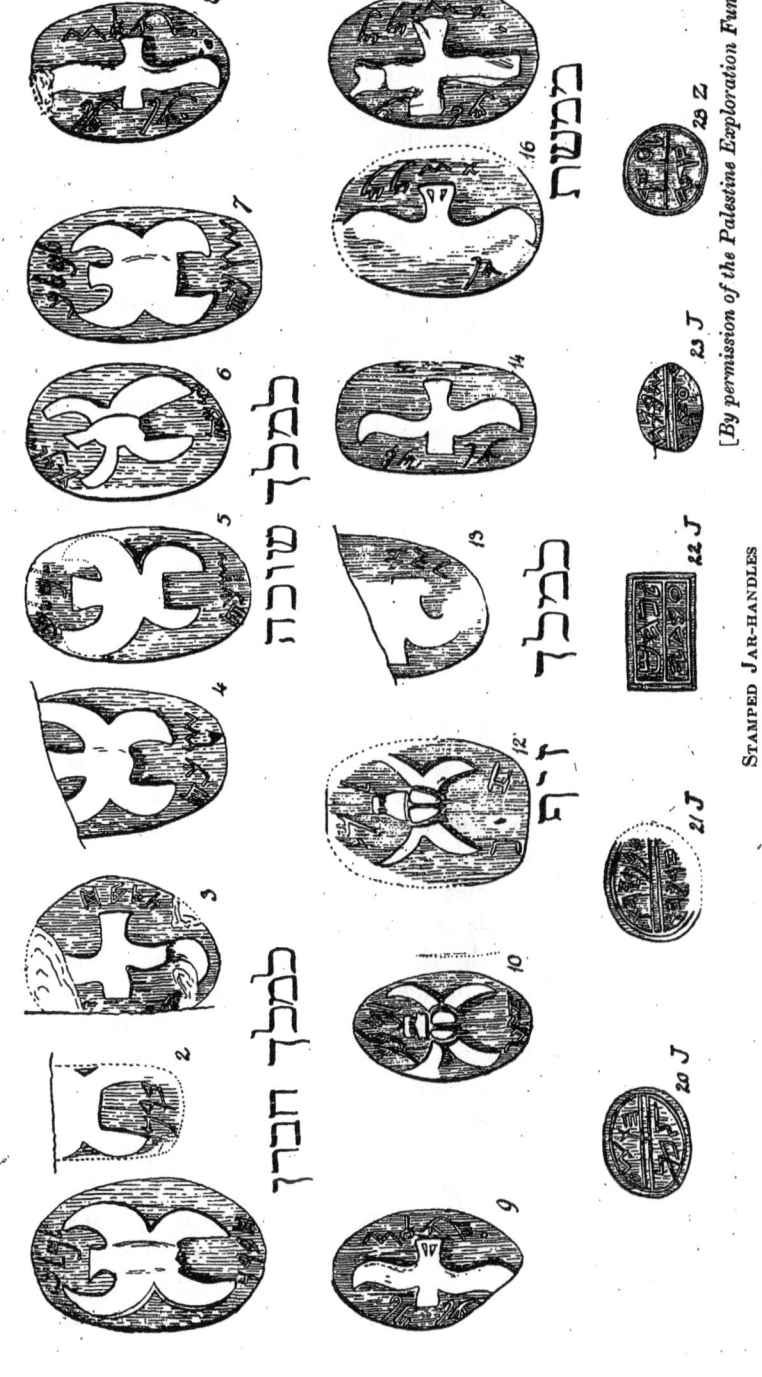

STAMPED JAR-HANDLES

[*By permission of the Palestine Exploration Fund.*]

was under the rule of a number of petty local kings—the kings of Hebron, Lachish, Gezer, Beth-el, &c. (Joshua xii. 9-24). Further consideration, however, of the position of the débris in which the handles were found soon made it evident that they could not be of this early date, but that they must belong to the period of the Jewish monarchy. What, then, was the meaning of the legends, 'Of (or For) the king. Hebron,' 'Of (or For) the king. Ziph,' &c.? Professor Sayce suggested[1] that they indicated that the vessels to which the handles belonged were made at potteries belonging to the king, and worked as royal monopolies, situated at the places named; and he pointed in confirmation of this view to the curious passage in 1 Chron. iv. 23 which speaks apparently of royal potteries: 'These were the potters, and the inhabitants of Netaim and Gederah: with the king in his work they dwelt there.' M. Clermont-Ganneau[2] supposed that the jars in question were receptacles, officially gauged and stamped beforehand, for the collection, by the authorities of the towns whose names were stamped upon the handles, of dues and taxes payable to the king in kind from the surrounding districts. Upon either theory, it remains some difficulty that, among some fifty handles, found at four or (including Jerusalem) five different places, the names of only four towns should appear. In 1902, in the *Excavations in Palestine*, Dr. Bliss accepted the royal-pottery theory, thinking that the district in which the jar-handles were found was one likely to be supplied with ware from potteries in the four places named. Mr. Macalister, on the other hand, accepted then M. Clermont-Ganneau's theory, accounting for the geographical distribution of the jars by the supposition that, after the produce was delivered at Jerusalem, they became the perquisites of the tax-gatherers, who sold them to any one who would buy them; and explaining the occurrence of the four names only upon the same principle as Dr. Bliss, viz. that the purchasers from the towns represented by the sites excavated would naturally deal with the tax-gatherers of the neighbouring districts. The native foreman of the works[3] suggested an explanation, supported by modern usage in Palestine, that the jars were measures of capacity, which varied locally—as measures and weights vary now locally in Palestine—and that the stamp was the official royal recognition of the local standard of the place named. On the whole, with our present knowledge, the opinion that the jars were made at a royal pottery seems the most satisfactory, especially if we suppose with Père Vincent[4] that the royal stamp was at the same time a guarantee

---

[1] *QS.* 99. 210.
[2] *QS.* 99. 206 f.
[3] *Excavations in Palestine*, p. 114 f.
[4] *Canaan*, p. 359.

of the capacity of the jar to which it was attached. The supposition that the royal stamp was a guarantee of capacity, it will have been noticed, is an element in three of these theories: whether it is correct can only be definitely established when a sufficient number of unbroken jars have been recovered, and their capacity measured. Père Vincent points out that the neighbourhood of Hebron and Beit-jibrin is rich in clay adapted for the manufacture of pottery, and that large jars, bowls, and dishes made at these places are at this day preferred in Jerusalem to other makes. High as my respect for Mr. Macalister is, I am sorry that I cannot at all accept his later theory[1] that Hebron, Ziph, Socoh, and Mamshith are the names, not of towns, but of the royal potters themselves, and that they actually occur as such in 1 Chron. ii and iv. Mamshith does not occur at all in Chronicles; and the other names, where they do occur, are as clearly as possible the names of towns. All the other inferences drawn by Mr. Macalister on the subject, whether as developed in his articles in the *Quarterly Statement*,[2] or as summarized in the chapter (pp. 149 ff.) in *Bible Side-Lights from the Mound of Gezer* on the 'Craftsmen of Judah', are speculations based (as a comparison of the parallel texts printed on pp. 153-5 of the last-named work is surely sufficient to show) upon either a far-fetched exegesis or arbitrary alterations of the text: in the *Quarterly Statement*[3] he describes them himself, very justly, as a 'string of conjectures'. There is a reasonable possibility that the jar-handles in question may have been, as Professor Sayce and others have suggested, the work of the king's potters mentioned in 1 Chron. iv. 23; beyond this, with our present evidence, we cannot go.

I may add that there were found at Sandaḥannah, from the Greek period, a large number (328) of wine-jars from Rhodes, each stamped with two out of the three following items: the name of the Rhodian priest or eponymous magistrate of the year in which the jar was made; the month of his year of office; and the name of the merchant, probably the wine-merchant, who supplied it.[4]

[1] *QS.* 05. 243 ff., 328 ff.

[2] 'Father', in these genealogies, evidently means *founder*, or settler. We read, for instance, of the 'father' of Beth-zur, Kiriath-jearim, Beth-lehem, and Beth-gader (1 Chron. ii. 45, 50, 51), of Tekoa, Eshtemoa (1 Sam. xxx. 28), and Keilah (1 Chron. iv. 5, 17, 19): will it be seriously contended that these are all the names of persons? There are many other examples (e.g. Gen. x, xxv. 13-15), showing clearly that in genealogies the Hebrews were accustomed to represent places, tribes, and populations as individuals. And can 'the sons of Bithiah [a proper name, meaning, apparently, 'Daughter of Yah'], the daughter of Pharaoh' be reasonably interpreted as signifying 'men who used the scarabaeus' (*QS.* 05. 252)? [3] *QS.* 05. 341.

[4] Numerous Rhodian jar-handles have also been found at Gezer (*QS.* 09. 18).

These stamps have all been carefully described and tabulated by Mr. Macalister in the *Quarterly Statement*, 1901, pp. 28 ff., 124 ff. (cf. also the list of decipherable inscriptions in *Excavations in Palestine*, pp. 132-4). They are of interest as evidence of the trade in wine with Rhodes carried on during the third and second centuries B. C., and also as affording information respecting the Rhodian calendar, and the series of Rhodian eponymous magistrates.

I must now call attention to the two cuneiform tablets found on the west hill of Gezer in the sixth stratum.[1] The tablets are imperfectly preserved; but enough remains to show that they are contracts, one for the sale of a field, the other for the sale of an estate, with a house, land, and (probably) slaves; and the names of the owners, of the witnesses before whom the deeds were executed, and of the eponymous rulers who fix the dates, are all clearly legible. The dates correspond to 651 and 648 B.C., in the reign of Manasseh of Judah (698-641), and of Asshurbanipal of Assyria (668-625): one is dated by the name of a viceroy (*shaknu*) of Carchemish: the name of one of the owners is Hebrew (Nethaniah), those of the two joint-owners of the estate in the other case, and of the witnesses (twelve altogether) in both cases, are nearly all Assyrian—certainly none of those preserved is Hebrew. The contracts are drawn up in the form usual in Assyrian tablets. The exact historical significance of these tablets can hardly be established without further evidence; but they may be taken to show at least that there was an Assyrian colony settled at Gezer, and, perhaps, a garrison stationed there. Both Asshurbanipal and his predecessor Esarhaddon, it is to be remembered, in their lists of tributary kings of the West, mention Manasseh of Judah by the side of the kings of Gaza, Ashkelon, Ekron, and Ashdod, as also of the kings of Tyre, Edom, Moab, and Ammon; and these two tablets may be an indication of the Assyrian domination of Judah at the time, which is also not improbably alluded to in Nahum i. 13, 15, where the prophet promises Judah speedy deliverance from the yoke of Nineveh.

In 1904 a very interesting discovery was made in Gezer, relating to the Maccabaean period. It was the age in which Antiochus Epiphanes, king of Syria (175-164 B.C.), sought to unite all peoples of his empire in the worship of Olympian Zeus, and to abolish all local worships. Accordingly the Jews were required to give up all the practices of their own religion, and to sacrifice to Zeus, under pain of death. Many of the Hellenizing Jews conformed to these re-

[1] *QS.* 04. 207 f., 229-37 (T. G. Pinches), 237-43 (C. H. W. Johns); 05. 185, 206-10 (Johns), 272 (A. H. Sayce).

quirements; but a stout resistance was made by the loyal Jews, led first by Mattathias, a priest of Modin, a town eighteen miles north-west of Jerusalem, and continued by his son Judas Maccabaeus, who gained many brilliant victories, and re-dedicated the temple in 165 B.C. (1 Macc. iv.), and after his death by his brothers Jonathan and Simon.[1] We learn now, from 1 Macc. ix. 52, that in the course of the contest with the Jews, the Syrian general Bacchides, in 161 B.C., seized and fortified Gezer, as a stronghold against the Jews; and from 1 Macc. xiii. 43-8, that some years afterwards, in 143 B.C., Simon succeeded in recovering it, expelled the Syrians from it, placed in it loyal Israelites, and built in it a palace for himself.

In 1904[2] the wall along the south of the mound was being traced under Mr. Macalister's direction, when it was found that just at the point where it should cross the central depression, there was a gap of nearly 300 feet, without any signs of the wall being continued through it. After further excavation, however, there appeared traces of a wall, running from east to west, both north and south of this gap; and also, soon afterwards, of two well-constructed gateways in these two walls, with a pavement of cobble-stones, leading up into the city, between them.[3] As these walls were not part of the city walls, it was argued that they must belong to some important building, such as a castle, near them; and as, moreover, the gateway leading into the city was in it, that it must have been under the control of some one who had the right to pass in and out of the city at his pleasure, i.e. of a military governor of the city. The pottery associated with the gateways was of Maccabaean date; and accordingly Mr. Macalister was led to think it not improbable that the castle was the building spoken of in 1 Macc. xiii. 48 as erected for himself by Simon.

For the time this supposition was merely a hypothesis: it lacked proof. One day, one of the basket-girls picked up a fragment of building-stone, from near the outer wall, with some characters inscribed upon it, and brought it to Mr. Macalister. The characters were Greek; and though parts are not quite certain, two words of interest in it are, and these are, 'Simon's palace': '(Says) Pampras: *May fire pursue Simon's palace!*'[4] The words are an imprecation, uttered by some Syrian, that fire may destroy the

---

[1] See for particulars Lect. III in E. Bevan's *Jerusalem under the High-Priests* (1904), five admirably written lectures on the period between Nehemiah and the New Testament.

[2] *QS.* 05. 97 ff.   [3] See the plan, ibid., opposite p. 104.

[4] Ibid., 101, 184. The word rendered 'pursue' is uncertain.

palace built by Simon. The inscription constitutes, not perhaps a proof, but still a strong presumption that Mr. Macalister's supposition was correct; and that the building thus disinterred at the gate of the city was in reality the palace built by Simon.

Afterwards, as M. Clermont-Ganneau showed from Josephus,[1] the city passed again into Syrian hands, and Simon's work was undone. The castle was plundered, and ruined to its foundations; and over at least part of it was built an elaborate system of baths consisting of seven chambers, all but one paved and lined with cement, containing tanks, a furnace for heating water, and other connected rooms.[2]

I have alluded before to Professor Sellin's excavations at Taanach; and it may be interesting now to give an outline of the principal results obtained by him. Taanach lies on a hill close in front of the range which bounds on the south-west the broad plain of Esdraelon, or, as it is called in the Old Testament, the plain of Megiddo. Five miles north-west of it is Tell el-Mutesellim, which was excavated afterwards by Dr. Schumacher, in all probability the site of the ancient Megiddo. Between these two places passed the regular ancient route for both caravans and armies from Babylon and Damascus to Gaza and Egypt.[3] Both, especially Megiddo, were thus alike commercially and strategically important; and both are often mentioned together. They are first named in history by Thothmes III (1503-1447), who enumerates them by the side of many other towns in Palestine, as captured by him on his expedition into Syria. In Joshua xii. 21 the kings of both Taanach and Megiddo are included in the list of thirty-one smitten by Joshua. Neither place was, however, occupied by the Israelites; in Joshua xvii. 11 (= Judges i. 27) they are mentioned as two of a belt of fortresses extending from Beth-shean to Dor, from which the tribe of Manasseh was unable to expel the Canaanites, and thus isolating the Hebrews of the north of Palestine from those of the centre. In the Song of Deborah, 'Taanach by the waters of Megiddo'—i.e. probably some of the streams running down past it from the hills into the Kishon—is named as a spot near which the 'kings of Canaan', with their army, were swept away before the rising Kishon (Judges v. 19-21). In Solomon's time Taanach and Megiddo were centres of one of the administrative districts established by the king (1 Kings iv. 12); and

---

[1] Cf. *QS*. 05. 113.

[2] *QS*. 05. 110-12 (with plans and view, Plate II, and p. 108 f.); *Side-Lights from the Mound of Gezer*, p. 196 (view).

[3] *Mitteilungen und Nachrichten des Deutschen Pal.-Vereins*, 1903, pp. 4 ff.

VIEW OF TELL TA'ANNEK FROM THE NORTH
From *Tell Ta'annek* (1904), p. 10 (Fig. 2).

To face p. 80]

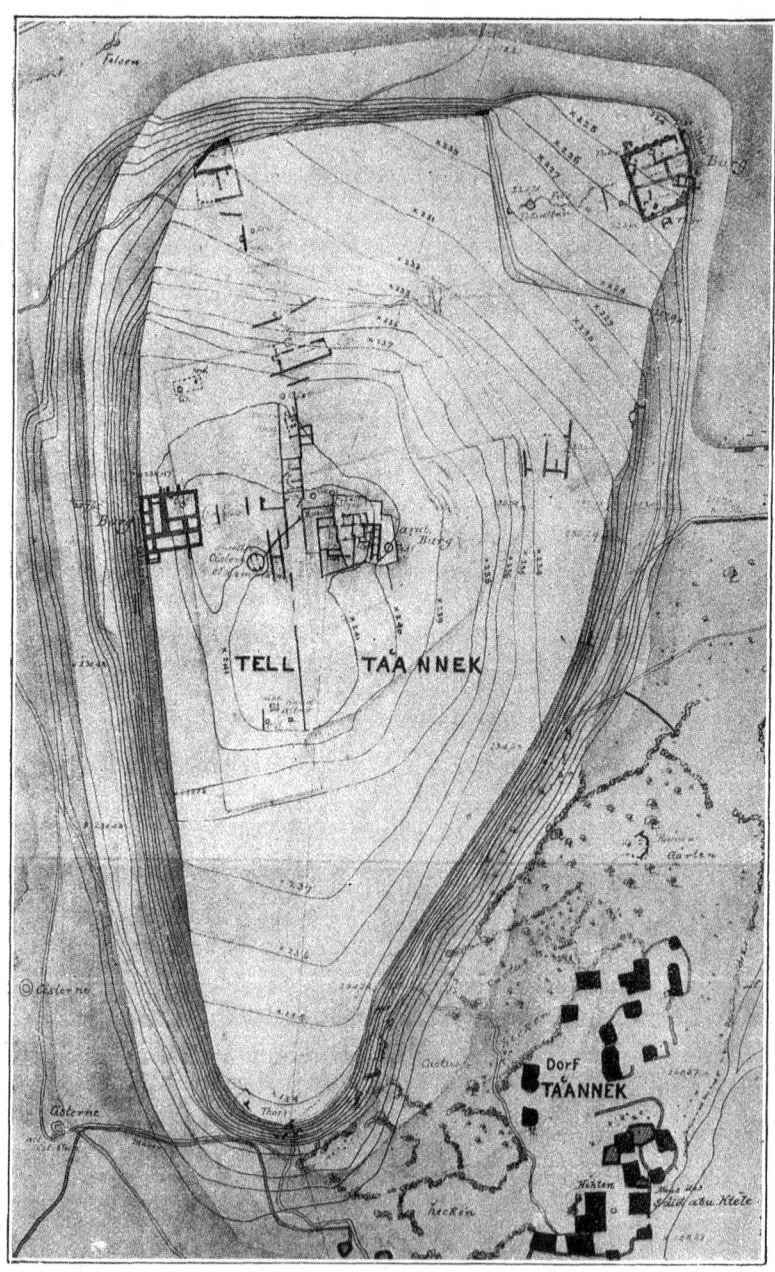

PLAN OF TELL TA'ANNEK

Reduced from the Plan at the end of *Tell Ta'annek*. The figures give the height in metres (1 metre = 39·37 inches) above the sea. The traces of Ishtar-washur's residence may be seen faintly to the south-west of the north-east fortress, near the isometric figure 233.

Megiddo is also stated to have been fortified by him (1 Kings ix. 15). Under Jeroboam I Shishak tells us that he plundered Taanach in his invasion of Palestine (cf. 1 Kings xiv. 25, 26).

In the excavation of Taanach [1] no traces were found, except perhaps some empty caves, of the neolithic cave-dwellers, such as were revealed by the excavations at Gezer. Professor Sellin holds that pottery gives the key to the archaeology of Palestine; and he regards our knowledge of its importance for this purpose as dating from the epoch-making work of Professor Petrie on Tell el-Ḥesy. He accordingly arranges the history of Taanach into four periods (1, 2, 3, 4), each being subdivided into two sections (a, b), characterized by different types of pottery. The first section of the first

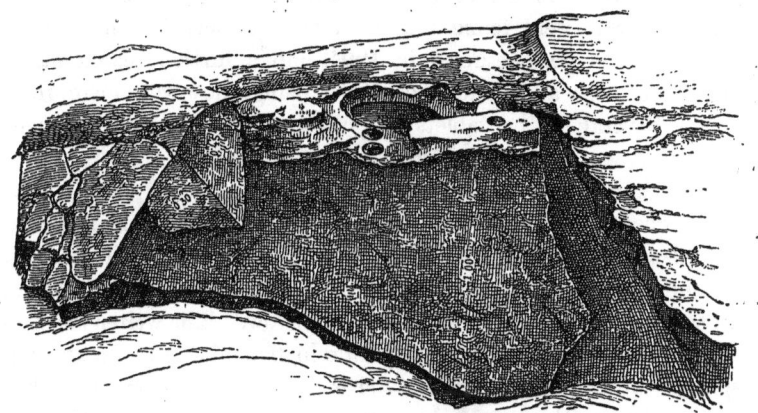

CANAANITE ROCK-ALTAR AT TAANACH

From Kittel, *Studien zur hebräischen Archäologie und Religionsgeschichte*, p. 134 (reduced from *Tell Ta'annek*, fig. 31, p. 34).

period (1 a) extends from about 2000 to 1300 B.C.: [2] it is marked by the advent of the first people who have left clear traces of their presence at Taanach, the Canaanites, who appear similarly at about the same time, or a little earlier, at Gezer. The pottery is the same as that of the corresponding period in Southern Palestine. A rock-hewn altar, with one large and three small cup-shaped cavities on the top, showing that it was intended for libations and not for sacrifice (pp. 34, 36, 103 [3]), and with a step leading up to it, hewn out

---

[1] For the titles of the two books in which Prof. Sellin's excavations are described, see above p. 10, note 3.

[2] See *Eine Nachlese*, &c., p. 31 (against *Tell Ta'annek*, p. 102, where 1 a is regarded as ending at B.C. 1600, and B.C. 1600–1300 are referred to 1 b).

[3] Here and in the sequel the references in the text are to the pages of Sellin's *Tell Ta'annek*.

of the rock, belongs also to the same period. Four yards behind this altar were found four jar-buried infants, and also the skeleton of an adult, close by a large jug and a broken saucer; not far off, also, sixteen more jar-buried infants (pp. 33, 34). A large fortified building towards the north of the Tell, intended apparently as a governor's residence, dates probably from the latter part of the same period.

An unexpected discovery, made in this building, gave a welcome glimpse into the internal condition of Taanach in, or perhaps a few years after, the Tell el-Amarna period (c. 1350 B.C.). In one of the chambers of the building there was found a large rectangular clay chest, which had been used, as soon appeared, for the storage of official archives. It fell to pieces when it was moved; but either in it or near it were found four cuneiform tablets, to which, when the excavations were resumed in 1904, and a further search made, eight more were added, four of these being, however, mere fragments. Several of the tablets are unhappily mutilated; but even what remains of them is of great interest. Four are addressed to Ishtar-washur, the king or ruler of Taanach at the time. One, a short one, I may quote[1]: 'To Ishtar-washur from Aman-ḥashir. May Adad preserve thy life! Send thy brethren with their chariots, and send a horse thy tribute, and presents, and all prisoners who are with thee; send them to Megiddo by to-morrow.' The writer was presumably some one in authority at Megiddo, five miles off. In another dispatch[2] Aman-ḥashir says that he is in Gaza, and complains that Ishtar-washur neither comes himself nor even sends his brother, or the expected troops, which he seems to imply are needed to defend him against his foes. A third[3] is from one Guli-adda. Ishtar-washur has written to tell him that he is in straits for want of money; and he promises to send him fifty pieces of silver. He continues: 'Everything that thou hast heard I have learnt through Belram. And if the finger of Ashirat shows itself, let them enforce and observe it.' We do not know what is alluded to; but the expression 'finger of Ashirat' is noticeable. 'Ashirat' is to all appearance the original of the Ashérah, or sacred post, of the Hebrews (above, p. 64); and though the name Abdashirta, 'servant of Ashirta,' in the Tell el-Amarna letters, implied that it was the name of a deity, this is the first time that she has been found expressly mentioned as such. The expression, 'finger of Ashirat,' refers doubtless to an oracle.[4]

[1] No. 5 (*Nachlese*, p. 36). [2] No. 6 (ibid. p. 37). [3] No. 1 (*Tell Ta'annek*, p. 113).
[4] For the use of the term 'finger' Dr. Langdon refers me to Behrens, *Ass.-Bab. Briefe kultischen Inhalts* (1906), p. 78.

Ishtar-washur's daughter, also, when she grows up, is to be given to 'royalty', and belong to the 'lord', i. e. apparently to enter the harem of the Pharaoh. Another letter,[1] from Aḥi-yami, alludes, rather obscurely, to some towns lost by Ishtar-washur—no doubt dependent towns in the plain of Megiddo, the 'daughters of Taanach' of Joshua xvii. 11 (= Judges i. 27); and we wonder whether, like so many of the governors in the Tell el-Amarna letters, he has been suffering from the Ḥabiri. The name Aḥi-yami (or -yawi), also, may be the same as the Hebrew Aḥiyah (Ahijah), i. e. 'Yah is a brother', and contain the name *Yahweh*. If so, how did the name get here? Is it another indication of Israelites settled in Canaan before the exodus under Moses? Let us hope that the discovery of further tablets may throw fuller light on these interesting questions. But whatever the true answer to these questions may be, it is remarkable to find two local chiefs, or governors, using Babylonian, not for official communications made to their over-lord in Egypt, but in private correspondence with each other. These cuneiform letters are eloquent testimony to the hold which Babylonian influence exercised over Canaan at the time: two neighbouring governors use Babylonian, to all appearance, as if it were their native tongue.[2]

In close connexion with this residence of Ishtar-washur there were found also two large subterranean caves, with a chamber in front of them hewn out of the rock, communicating by winding stairs, and also by a channel or conduit beside the stairs, with an altar above hewn out of the rock. There can be little doubt that this was an altar intended for sacrifices to the dead, the channel being intended to convey the blood into the caves, supposed to be the abode of the dead.[3]

The fort on the west, built of massive stone, and adapted in the interior to be the residence of a king or governor (pp. 52, 102), is shown by the superior style both of its architecture and of its pottery to be of later date than the residence of Ishtar-Washur,[4] and may be referred to the period 1 *b*. Eight figures of Astarte were also found, belonging either to the latter part of 1 *a* or to 1 *b* (p. 102).

We come to the second period, 1200–800 B.C. The first section of this period (2 *a*), 1200–1000 B.C., would include the first two centuries of the Hebrew occupation of Canaan, though, as we have

---

[1] No. 2 (*Tell Ta'annek*, p. 115). [2] Cf. *Tell Ta'annek*, p. 98 f.

[3] Cf. at Gezer (above, p. 51); and at Megiddo (p. 67).

[4] So Sellin, *Nachlese*, p. 31, modifying the opinion which he had expressed previously (*Tell Ta'annek*, p. 102).

seen, Taanach, like Gezer, remained throughout that time in the possession of the Canaanites. The second section (1000–800 B.C.) begins shortly before the reign of Solomon. Throughout this period Phoenician influence is markedly prominent in the pottery [1]; in the second section of the period (2 b) the influence of Egypt, and especially of Cyprus, is also perceptible. The jar-buried infants belong to either this or the preceding period (p. 97). The foundation sacrifices which begin in 1 b continue through 2 a. The two standing-stones, one with a hole in the top, and the other with one in its side, for libations, belong to the periods 2 a and 2 b (pp. 69, 104): they were thus presumably erected by Canaanites, and continued to be used by Israelites. The double row of ten *mazzēbāhs*, five in each row, under the north fort belong apparently to the second section of this period (2 b): they were thus probably erected by Israelites (pp. 18, 104). Two other *mazzēbāhs* (pp. 72, 105), standing each at the entrance of a private house, served probably as domestic altars: these belong to the periods 2 b and 3 a, and are consequently Israelitish. Ten figures of Astarte were also found, five belonging to each of the periods 2 a and 2 b. The north-east fort was erected during the period 2 b: Professor Sellin thinks probably by Solomon, or, if not by him, by one of the early North Israelite kings (p. 103). There is no evidence of a break, or abrupt change, in the civilization between the Canaanite and the Israelite occupation of Taanach: the excavations show rather gradual development. The Canaanites will have gradually assimilated the Israelites drawn to them from the villages in the plain (p. 102).

The third period, from 800–100 B.C., is that of Hellenic influence, naturally slighter at first, till in the Seleucid period it becomes predominant; but only the first part of it (3 a), to about 600 B.C., is represented at Taanach. The north-east fort was destroyed, perhaps at the ruin of the Northern Kingdom in 722; but the castle north-west of it must have been built soon afterwards in its place (p. 103). The city during this period extended more widely than before; remains of it are found nearly everywhere on the hill (p. 103). There are no signs of Assyrian influence in this period (ibid.); and only two figures of Astarte were found in it.[2] The most interesting find dating from this period was a curiously decorated movable incense-altar, made of terra-cotta.[3] When found, it was in not less than thirty-six fragments; but these happily could be pieced together without

---

[1] *Tell Ta'annek*, p. 91.
[2] In 1904 (*Nachlese*, pp. 33, 36; contrast *Tell Ta'annek*, p. 106).
[3] *Tell Ta'annek*, pp. 75 ff., 109 f.

Two Standing-stones at Taanach
From *Tell Ta'annek*, p. 69 (Fig. 87).

Double Row (one imperfect) of Standing-stones at Taanach
From *Tell Ta'annek*, p. 18 (Fig. 10).

[To face p. 84

TERRA-COTTA INCENSE-ALTAR FOUND AT TAANACH
Reduced from Plate XII at the end of *Tell Ta'annek*.

INCENSE-ALTAR FOUND AT TAANACH

difficulty. It was just 3 ft. high, and in shape roughly like a truncated pyramid, the four sides at the bottom being each 18 in. long, and the whole ending at the top in a bowl a foot in diameter. Along the two sides of the front there are three animal figures with wings and human heads, and between them two lions whose paws rest on the heads of the composite figures beneath them. The human heads have beardless faces, and sharp prominent noses, analogous to those of early Greek figures. The composite figures are probably intended for either sphinxes or cherubim. At the bottom there is a representation of a sacred tree. On the left side of the front there is a bas-relief of a boy throttling (or taming) a serpent, whose open jaws are extended towards him.[1] A sacred tree, with two animals—lions, sphinxes, or wild goats—beside it, is a representation found frequently in Cyprus, as also on Assyrian seals and Egyptian scarabs[2]; and the form of the sacred tree here resembles much two given by Ohnefalsch-Richter, *Cyprus*, Plates LXXVII. 17, CXVII. 7. The altar is hollow: when in use a fire was kindled on the ground, and the altar placed over it; the ascending draught[3] thus kept the fire alight, so that it heated the incense in the bowl at the top.[4] Professor Sellin places the date of the altar at about 700 B.C. One wonders whether the Israelites, who are so often said to have burnt incense on the mountains, used an altar of this kind for the purpose. This altar is also essentially a large and decorated Hebrew *tannūr*, or 'oven': did such an altar suggest the figure of the smoking *tannūr*, which, passing between the divided victims, symbolizes Yahweh in Gen. xv? An incense-altar of exactly the same shape (a stem broadening out towards the base), but of much smaller size, and made of pottery decorated simply by bands and triangles in black and red, has been found quite recently at Gezer in débris of about 1000-600 B.C. (*QS*. 08. 211). The cup at the top, and the base, are both gone; but there are remains of six pendant lotus leaves, which once encircled the stem just below the cup. The present height of the stem is $7\frac{3}{4}$ inches.

Some disaster, whether at the hands of the Scythians (*c*. 626 B.C.), or the Egyptians, when Pharaoh Neco defeated Josiah at Megiddo in

[1] The boy rather resembles the Cypriote beast-tamer, represented in Ohnefalsch-Richter, *Cyprus*, Plate CXVIII. 7*a*, CC. 4.

[2] Sellin (p. 78), citing Ohnefalsch-Richter, i. 74 ff.

[3] There are holes in the side of the altar, which would have the effect of creating a draught.

[4] Cf. ibid. CXXXV. 1ᵃ, 1ᵇ, 2 (a terra-cotta incense-dish, on the top of a hollow pedestal, broadening out slightly at the base, not unlike the incense-altar from Gezer, mentioned below on this page).

608, seems soon afterwards to have overtaken the city; for no remains, or at least no substantial remains, were found upon the Tell that could be dated between 600-500 B.C. and 900 A.D. (p. 103). The large village spoken of by Eusebius must have been situated not on the Tell itself, but on the plain at its foot. The castle at the top of the Tell, as the articles found in it, including an Arabic inscription, showed clearly, was built by the Arabs in about the tenth century of our era.

Let me in conclusion give a brief summary of the principal results gained from the excavations that have been now imperfectly outlined. All the sites excavated give evidence alike of the successive cities built upon them, and of the successive strata of population which inhabited them. The buildings and objects found enable us to draw with tolerable confidence many interesting conclusions respecting the civilization and religious and other practices of the people inhabiting them. At Gezer we learn first of a Neolithic, non-Semitic race, who dwelt in caves, and have left remains of their rude handiwork, dating from the period before the Canaanite immigration. Then we find a Canaanite civilization in Palestine lasting from c. 2000 to 1200 B.C.: this is recognizable especially by the pottery. Side by side with this we have traces of the very different Babylonian civilization, which it is evident influenced Canaan deeply during many centuries before the Hebrew occupation. The cuneiform inscriptions found at Tell el-Ḥesy and Taanach confirm and extend the conclusions authorized in this respect by the Tell el-Amarna letters. The scarabs and other articles of Egyptian origin found especially at Gezer give evidence of considerable intercourse between Egypt and at least the south-west of Canaan. For a century or two before the Israelite period the pottery found at both Gezer and Taanach testifies to the influence of the art and civilization of Phoenicia, Crete, the islands of the Aegean Sea, and Cyprus: in the eighth and seventh centuries B.C., also, at least some of the ware—whether native or imported, experts are not agreed—bears a Western character, and resembles strongly, for instance, that of Cyprus and Greece. During the Israelite period the character of the pottery deteriorates;[1] but at present opinions differ as to the date at which the deterioration begins. Babylonian influence ceases, after the Hebrew occupation, almost entirely. The contract tablets found at Gezer dating from 651 and 648 B.C. testify to the presence of Assyrians there at this time: probably, indeed, in both

[1] Sellin, *Der Ertrag der Ausgrabungen im Orient für die Erkenntnis der Entwicklung der Religion Israels* (1905), p. 28; cf. Vincent, p. 353.

SUMMARY OF RESULTS OF EXCAVATION 87

the eighth and seventh centuries B.C. the power of Assyria was more strongly felt in Canaan than would be supposed from the express statements of the Bible: the tribute of Jehu, for instance, though attested by the Black Obelisk of Shalmaneser, is not mentioned in the Book of Kings; and allusions in the prophets point in the same direction.

We see also in Palestine the same progress in civilization which we find in other countries: first stone used as implements, then bronze, then iron. At Gezer we have first the rough earth rampart, with stone facings, of the aboriginal Neolithic population, followed by the more massive stone walls built by subsequent occupiers. The usual sites for Canaanite towns were either on the projecting spur of a range of hills, like Gezer, Tell eṣ-Ṣāfi, and Megiddo, or on an isolated hill rising up out of the plain, such as Tell el-Ḥesy and Taanach. We can therefore understand how the Canaanite cities, standing thus on eminences, with substantial walls, such as excavation has revealed to us, must have impressed the Israelite invaders: the Hebrew traditions of the conquest still preserve recollections of the Canaanite cities being 'great' and 'fenced', i.e. fortified, or—to preserve the Hebrew metaphor—*cut off*, i.e. unapproachable by assailants, impregnable.[1]

The excavations show no trace of a break between the Canaanite and Israelite culture: there is no sudden change from one to the other; the transition is gradual.[2] This is in agreement with what appears from a careful study of the Old Testament itself. There was no extermination of the Canaanites on the scale represented in the later strata of the Book of Joshua, the writers of which, looking back upon the past, pictured the Israelite occupation of Canaan, as they knew it, as already complete in the lifetime of Joshua himself.[3] As other and earlier passages in the Books of Joshua and Judges show, the Israelite supremacy in Canaan was in fact gained far more gradually: the Canaanites in many places lived on side by side with the Israelites—in the case of Shechem we learn this from the Book of Judges itself (chap. ix); and the Israelites borrowed from them many elements of their civilization.

We learn also much about the religion of Canaan. First there is the sacred cave of the aboriginal Neolithic race, into which from the

---

[1] Num. xiii. 28; cf. Joshua xiv. 12. The rhetorical addition, 'up to heaven,' is found only in Deuteronomy (i. 28; ix. 1).

[2] Cf. Vincent, p. 463 f.; also pp. 204, 461, with note 3.

[3] See e. g. the generalizing summaries in Josh. xi. 40-42, xii. 16-23, xxi. 43-45; and contrast Josh. xiii. 1 *end* with the first chapter of Judges.

rock above offerings seem to have been sent down either to the dead or to subterranean deities. Then we find high places at Tell el-Ḥesy, Gezer, Taanach, and Megiddo, with the sacred standing-stones, and sometimes rock-altars beside them: of rock-altars, also, traces apparently exist in other parts of Palestine as well. The standing-stones are found in Israelite as well as Canaanite times, as indeed would naturally be expected from the Old Testament itself. Underneath the high place at Gezer have been found [1] memorials of the grim rites performed in honour of the *numen loci*—the bones of children which had been sacrificed, and sometimes burnt, and then deposited in jars. These jar-buried infants have also been found at Tell el-Mutesellim and Taanach. Instances after 1200 B.C. are, however, rare. When this practice was given up, the mere lamp and bowl seems to have been adopted as a symbolical substitute. Somewhat later, also, we find instances of foundation-sacrifices, or human sacrifices offered at the foundation of a house or other building, to secure the welfare of its future inhabitants. We may add to the instances already mentioned the skeleton of a child found in a large jar just a yard under the great altar-stone in the residence of Ishtar-washur.[2] Numerous figures of Ashtōreth or Astarte were also found, though these are rarer in Israelite than in Canaanite times. Professor Sellin mentions,[3] as illustrating current popular superstitions, the discovery at Taanach of a small jar containing sixty-six animal ankle-bones, fashioned into the shape of beans, to be used presumably as lots for ascertaining the will of a deity, many serpents' heads for use in incantations, two serpent-like bronze knives, and golden crescents (cf. Judges viii. 26), intended as amulets to ward off the evil eye. The incense-altar found at Taanach is also an evident monument of the popular Israelite religion.

We wish that Canaanite inscriptions had been found: but even without them, the Canaanites through all these discoveries—to use Professor Sellin's expression [4]—take flesh and blood before us, and we realize, much more vividly than it was possible to do before, what their beliefs and usages were.[5]

I hope that I have succeeded in giving in these lectures at least a general idea of the nature and value of research in its bearing upon the Bible. For more numerous illustrations from discoveries that

---

[1] See, however, p. 69 note.
[2] *Eine Nachlese*, p. 11; *Der Ertrag der Ausgrabungen*, &c., p. 31.
[3] *Der Ertrag*, &c., p. 33. [4] Ibid., pp. 33, 37.
[5] See more fully on this subject Stanley A. Cook, *The Religion of Ancient Palestine in the Second Millennium B.C., in the Light of Archaeology and the Inscriptions*, 1908 (in the series called 'Religions : Ancient and Modern').

had been made up to 1899 I may be allowed to refer to the survey given by myself for the Old Testament, and by Dr. Headlam for the New Testament, in the volume called *Authority and Archaeology*, edited by Mr. Hogarth in 1899. To understand properly an ancient literature such as that of the Bible we need all the help and light that we can get from whatever quarter—from philology, from criticism, both documentary and historical, from many special studies, such as geography, geology, botany, zoology, from the observation of customs in Bible lands, and also from archaeology. The special value of archaeology consists in the fact that it affords us, in most cases, contemporary evidence; and hence in a most welcome manner, as the case may be, illustrates, supplements, confirms, or corrects, statements or representations contained in the Bible. It co-operates with documentary—otherwise, though not very clearly, called 'higher'[1]— criticism, in helping us to distinguish narratives in the Bible which are contemporary with the events recorded from those which are of later date, thereby assisting us to place its different parts in their true historical perspective. We must, however, be on our guard against confusing, as is sometimes done, the *facts* of archaeology with the ingenious, but precarious, inferences or hypotheses sometimes founded upon them. Archaeology is moreover of value, as nothing else is, in enabling us to construct pictures of the civilizations by which Israel was surrounded—the imposing empires of Egypt, Babylon, and Assyria—perhaps before long we may be able to add the Hittites—and those of the smaller, but by no means unimportant, tribes or nations, neighbours of the Hebrews, in Arabia, Syria, and Phoenicia.

The discoveries of the last fifty years enable us to realize, as it was impossible to realize before, both the resemblances and the differences between Israel and its neighbours. On their material side there are

---

[1] The term 'higher criticism' is often misunderstood, and, consequently, misapplied. It may be worth while, therefore, to explain that 'higher criticism' is not, as seems sometimes to be supposed, an intensified and exaggerated form of ordinary criticism: it is a particular branch or department of criticism, which is so called, simply because, as compared with 'lower', or textual, criticism, it deals with higher and more difficult problems; and its province is exclusively to determine, with the help of all the *data* available, the origin, date, and (if they are composite) literary structure of books, or parts of books. It is a mistake to suppose, as is sometimes done, that questions relating to history, the credibility of narratives, the origin and growth of religious beliefs, the influence of Babylonia upon Israel, &c., fall within the province of 'higher criticism'. The introduction of the expression into Biblical studies dates from the time of Eichhorn (1780): see C. A. Briggs, *General Introduction to the Study of Holy Scripture* (1899), p. 280.

many resemblances: the Hebrews were a Semitic people, and shared with their neighbours many similar laws, institutions, customs, and beliefs; in art, also, as the excavations have especially shown, they borrowed much from the civilizations about them: but religiously, there was a great gulf fixed, which, if possible, has been widened rather than narrowed by the new knowledge which has come to us. There was in Babylonia an extensive religious literature, there were temples, and priests, and sacrifices, there were prayers and hymns,— some, notably those of Nebuchadnezzar, marked by great elevation of thought,—there were even penitential psalms; but while in Babylonia, as elsewhere (Acts xvii. 27), there were, no doubt, seekers after God, if haply they might feel after Him and find Him, yet to the masses religion was polytheistic; the priests were often mere exorcisers, diviners, and soothsayers; magic, and a most superstitious use of oracles and omens, filled a great part in the religious life of the people: religious institutions and religious practices were not in Babylonia, as in Israel, made the vehicle and exponent of pure spiritual truths; there were no really spiritual teachers, such as the prophets were. Archaeology demonstrates, and shows us more clearly than we could see before, that though the religion of Israel was built upon the same material foundation as those of other Semitic peoples, it rose immeasurably above them; it assumed, as it developed, a unique character, and in the hands of its inspired teachers became the expression of great spiritual realities such as has been without parallel in any other nation of the earth.[1]

I need hardly, after what I have placed before you, insist specially on the importance and value of excavation. Some of the conclusions that have been reached are conjectural, or more or less provisional: we want to know whether further knowledge will confirm or correct them. There are historical and other questions on which we would gladly have further light: and excavation on fresh sites may give it

[1] The question of the influence of Babylonia upon the religion of Israel is too large to enter into here. In the opinion of the present writer, the influence was real, but not extensive, and confined to externals. Thus the *form* of the creation-story in Gen. i, which is in irreconcilable conflict with the teachings of science, is, for instance, derived from Babylonia, but the *spirit*, and religious teaching, with which it is infused, are purely Hebraic; the word 'sabbath' is of Babylonian origin, but 'the great social and religious institution which it represents in Israel is not Babylonian, but distinctively Hebrew'; in Job ix. 13 there is probably an allusion to a myth of Babylonian origin. For an instructive and interesting consideration of the question, with many translations of representative Babylonian texts, the reader may be referred to Prof. R. W. Rogers's Five Lectures on *The Religion of Assyria and Babylonia, especially in its relation to Israel* (New York), which has just appeared (Dec. 1908).

SUMMARY OF RESULTS OF EXCAVATION 91

us. We would gladly, if we could, discover some native Canaanite or Hebrew inscriptions.[1] We would gladly recover further monuments of Canaanite or Israelite practices and beliefs. The results which have already been obtained from excavation in Palestine are more than enough to encourage us to expect still more in the future. Biblical students cannot be too grateful to those who have thrown themselves into the work—to Professor Petrie, who inaugurated it; to Dr. Bliss and Mr. Macalister, who continued it, and the latter of whom at Gezer has displayed an energy, and resourcefulness, and skill, which are beyond all praise; and to Professor Sellin and Dr. Schumacher, who have done independently most admirable work at Taanach and Megiddo. Our good wishes will follow these two skilful explorers in their work at Jericho and Samaria, in which, as I have said before, they are now respectively engaged: Samaria, especially, on a large oblong hill, now with open fields at the top, but for a century and a half the wealthy and luxurious capital[2] of the Northern Kingdom, offers, as I could not help thinking myself when I stood upon the hill in 1888, a peculiarly promising site for the discovery of inscriptions. And I close with the earnest hope that the Palestine Exploration Fund, in which we in England are most nearly interested, may be kept provided with the necessary means of retaining the help and services of Mr. Macalister for many years to come.[3]

THE LION-SEAL FOUND AT MEGIDDO

Legend : לשמע עבד ירבעם, 'Belonging to Shama', servant of Jeroboam (i.e., not impossibly, King Jeroboam II, c. B.C. 783–743).

From *Tell el-Mutesellim*, p. 99 (Fig. 147).

---

[1] Since this sentence was in type, a Hebrew inscription has been found at Gezer. It consists of eight short lines, and is apparently a kind of calendar, describing the agricultural operation characteristic of each of eight months. It is written in a bold and clear hand, and may date from the eighth century B.C. A detailed account will be found in the *Quarterly Statement* for Jan. 1909.

[2] Cf. Amos vi. 1–6.

[3] A most interesting preliminary report of the excavations carried on upon the site of the ancient Jericho between Jan. 2 and Apr. 8, 1908, has just appeared in the *Mitteilungen der Deutschen Orient-Gesellschaft*, No. 39 (Dec. 1908). Tell es-Sultan, which now marks the site of the ancient city, is a long oval mound, about 1,100 ft. long and 500 ft. broad, with an average height of

40 ft. above the surrounding plain, and with seven smaller mounds rising up 16–40 ft. above it: it lies in the Jordan valley, 700 ft. below the Mediterranean Sea, five miles west of the river, very near the foot of the hills leading up into Judah; and the copious and beautiful 'Ain es-Sultan, or Elisha's Spring, wells up close to it on the east. At the close of the operations, a semicircular section of the wall, nearly 800 ft. in length, had been excavated at the north end of the oval, and a similar section of about 500 ft. at its south end, leaving some 1,200 ft. to be still excavated on its two sides. Towards the north end of the Tell, the northern part of the citadel, with a double protecting wall in front of it, was also excavated. The walls were in a singularly good state of preservation; and the excavators were astonished at their excellent workmanship and strength. The outer wall, surrounding the entire mound, consists of three parts. First the natural rock is overlaid with a filling of loam and fine gravel, 3–4 ft. deep; and upon this is built a sloping rubble wall, bulging outwards, $6\frac{1}{2}$–8 ft. thick and some 16 ft. high. The stones composing the rubble are large, and in the lower layers very large; the interstices are carefully filled in with smaller stones, so as to leave no space open for the insertion of any implement of destruction. This rubble wall is surmounted by a wall of brick, 6 ft. 6 in. thick, and now about 8 ft. high, though once probably considerably higher. The massive character of the outer wall of Jericho is well shown in the illustrations accompanying the report (pp. 6, 17). The citadel and its protecting walls are of hardly less substantial workmanship. The walls and citadel belong all to the Canaanite period; and the city must at that time have presented an imposing appearance, dominating the whole plain for many miles round. Within the citadel were found the walls and rooms of Canaanite houses, with remains of Canaanite pottery, and in many cases with infants buried in jars under the clay floors. On the south-east of the Tell, a little above the spring, was found a collection of Israelite houses, dating from about B.C. 700, and belonging consequently to the re-settlement of Jericho which began under Ahab (1 Kings xvi. 34). Numerous domestic utensils were discovered in these houses—plates and dishes, pots and *amphorae*, jugs and flagons, corn-mills of red sandstone, lamps and torch-holders, and many kinds of iron implements. The pottery is clearly related to the Graeco-Phoenician pottery found in Cyprus, and is quite unlike the ancient Canaanite ware. Rhodian (above, p. 77 f.) and other inscribed jar-handles were found, including one with the legend 'Of the king. Socoh' (above, p. 74). Prof. Sellin (p. 41) sums up the main results which have been at present attained as follows: (1) Jericho in the Canaanite period must have been an exceptionally strongly fortified place; (2) the development of its civilization shows a break, such as has not been observed elsewhere in Palestine, and after its Canaanite walls were partially demolished, it must for long have remained garden or arable land; and (3) the Egyptian and Aegean influence, traceable in its works of art, is not nearly as marked as it is in the cities of the west and north of Canaan.

INDEX

Abdi-ḫiba, governor of Jerusalem, 35-6, 44, 47.
Aegean art, influence of, on art in Palestine, 59, 86, 92.
Amorites, 36; meaning of term 'Amorite' as applied to pottery, 36.
Archaeology, value of, 89.
Ashérah, 64, 82.
Ashtōreth-Karnaim, 58.
Ashtōreth or Astarté, cult of, in Canaan, Phoenicia, and elsewhere, 56-9, 83, 84.
Asshur, excavation of city of, 30.
Asshur-banipal, library of, 6.
Assyrian inscriptions, often illustrate the Old Testament, 17-21.
Assyrian tablet found at Tell el-Ḥesy, 42, 44.
Assyrian tablets found at Gezer, 78.

Babylonian influence on Palestine and Asia Minor, 15-16, 27, 31, 33-4, 37, 82-3, 90.
Behistun Inscription read by Rawlinson, 4, 5.
Belshazzar, 25.
Bevan, E., 79 n.
Biblical Greek, the term a misnomer, 14; light thrown upon it from papyri and inscriptions, 14-15.
Black Obelisk, the, 16-17.
Bliss, Dr. F. J., *The Development of Palestine Exploration*, 8; excavates Tell el-Ḥesy, 10, 41 ff.
Bliss and Macalister excavate in south-west of Judah, 10, 74; particulars of their work given in *Excavations in Palestine*, 74 n., 76.
Boghaz-keui, excavations at, 31, 38.
Bronze, the metal used before iron, 44, 69, 87.
Burial-caves at Gezer, 50, 53-4, 54, 56.

Canaan an Egyptian province in the 15th cent. B.C., 33, 36; Babylonian spoken in, 33-4.
Cave-dwellers in Gezer, 51, 52.
Caves, sacred subterranean, 54, 67, 83; supposed oracular caves, 64-5.
Champollion, decipherer of Egyptian hieroglyphics, 3.
Children, sacrifice of, 68 9.
Classical archaeology, modern discoveries in, 2-3.
Clermont-Ganneau, 46.
Cook, Stanley A., on the Code of Hammurabi, 27 n.; on the Religion of ancient Palestine, p. 88 n.
Cooke, G. A., *North-Semitic Inscriptions*, 8 n.
Corn-grinder, primitive. 52.
Cos, sacrificial calendar of, 14-15.
Creation Tablets, 22-3.
Cuneiform inscriptions, decipherment of, 6-7.
Cuneiform tablets found at Tell el-Ḥesy, 42, 44; at Gezer, 78; at Taanach, 82-3.
Cup-marks on rocks, 51, 65, 67, 81.
Cyrus, 24-5.

Dalman, G., *Petra und seine Felsheiligtümer*, 61.
Darius the Mede, 25.
Deissmann, Prof. A., 2, 14.
Deluge Tablets, 22-3.

Egyptian hieroglyphics, decipherment of, 3-4.
Elephantine, papyri from, 28-30.
Ephesus, inscriptions from, 23-4.
Eponym Canon corrects Biblical dates, 20-1.
Erman, *Life in Ancient Egypt*, 4 n.
Evans, Dr. A. J., 2.

Foundation-sacrifices, 69-72, 88.
Frazer, Prof. J. G., quoted, 69 n.

Gezer, site of, 46 f.; earliest mention of, 47; Biblical notices of, 47, 49; excavations at, 49-80; excavation of first and second strata of, 49-52, third and fourth, 53-69, fifth and sixth, 69-74, 78, seventh, 78-80; earliest population of, 49; primitive earth rampart of, 51; walls of, 54-6; Canaanite castle in, 56; worship of Ashtōreth at, 56-7; cuneiform inscriptions found at, 78.
Gibeon, high place of, 66, 67.
Goshen, 26.
Greek inscriptions, collections of, 2.
Grenfell, Dr. B. P., 14.

Ḥabiri, the, 34, 35-6.
Ḥammurabi, 7; his code of laws, 26-7; his date, 26, 34 n.
Hebrew philology, growth of, 11-14.
High places in the Old Testament, 60-1; at Petra, 61-2; at Gezer, 62-5; remains of in Palestine now, 65-7.
'Higher criticism', meaning of the expression, 89 n.

Hincks, Edw., services to Assyriology, 5, 17, 19, 20.
Historical results of excavations, 86-7; as regards religion, 87-90.
Hittites, at Boghaz-keui, in the ancient Cappadocia, 31; correspond with Egyptian king in Babylonian, 31; conclude treaty with Egypt, 33, 37-8.
Hogarth, D. G., *The Penetration of Arabia*, 7 n.; editor of *Authority and Archaeology*, 16 n., 89.
Hunt, Dr. A. S., 14.

Incense-altar found at Taanach, 84-5; at Gezer, 85.
Infants buried in jars, supposed to have been sacrificed, at Gezer, 68-9; Megiddo, 68-9; Taanach, 68, 82, 84; found under a floor, 70, 92.
Inscriptions, value of, for history, 2-8; examples, 16-26, 30-1, 32 ff. Inscriptions:—Latin, 2; Greek, 2; Egyptian, 3-4, 26, 33, 36, 37-8, 38-9; Hittite, 31; Semitic, 7, 8:—Aramaic, 8 n., 28-30; Assyrian and Babylonian, 3-7, 17-21, 22-3, 24-7, 32-7, 38, 42, 44, 78, 82-3; Hebrew, 91 n.; Moabite, 21; Phoenician, 7; Sabaean and Minaean, 7 n.
Iron, period of first appearance of, at Tell el-Ḥesy, 44; at Gezer, 69.
Ishtar-washur, ruler of Taanach, cuneiform letters to, 82-3.
Israel, earliest mention of, in inscriptions, 39.

Jacob-el, 39.
Jar-handles, stamped, 74-7, 92.
Jehu, named on Black Obelisk of Shalmaneser II, 17.
Jericho, the rebuilding of, by Hiel, 72; excavation of the site of, 91-2.
Jerusalem, letters from the governor of, in the Tell el-Amarna correspondence, 35, 36.
'Job's Stone', 38.
Joseph-el, 39.
Judah tributary to Assyrians, 21, 78.

Kadesh-barnea, 9.
Kal'at Sherkāt, excavations at, 30.
Kenyon, Dr. F. G., 2 n., 11 n., 14 n.
King, L. W., 7, 23, 26.
Kittel, Prof. Rud., *Studien zur hebräischen Archäologie*, 64, 65 n., 66-7, 81.

Lachish, 45-6.
Lamp and bowl deposits in graves, 72-3.
Layard, A. H., 5, 6.
Levitical cities, 47 n.
Lidzbarski, M., 8.

Macalister, R. A. S., excavator of Gezer, 49-80 *passim*.
Maccabaean castle at Gezer, 78-9.
Mamshith, 74.

Maspero, G., 7 n.
Maẓẓēbāhs, 62.
Megiddo, 80-1, 82; mentioned by Thothmes III, 33.
Merenptah, 38-9; mentions Gezer, 47.
Mesha, king of Moab, inscription of, 21-2.
Mizpah, high place of, 66 f.
Moabite Stone, the, 21.
Mohar, *The Travels of a*, 38.
Mommsen, Prof. Theodor, 2 n.
Mond, Dr. Robert, 28.
Moulton, J. H., Lexical Notes from the Papyri, 15 n.

Naville, M., determines the sites of Pithom and Goshen, 26.
Neolithic age, remains of, at Gezer, 49, 51, 53.
New Testament, the Greek of the, illustrated by recent discoveries, 14-15.

Ordnance Survey of Palestine, 9.

Palaeolithic remains found near Gezer, 53.
Palästina-Verein, establishment of the, 9.
Palestine Exploration Fund, foundation of the, 9.
Palestine, maps of, 9.
Papyri, importance of, 2, 15 n.
Pergamum, inscriptions from, 14.
Perrot and Chipiez, *History of Art in Phoenicia and Cyprus*, 57 n., 59 n.
Petrie, Prof. Flinders, excavates in Egypt and Palestine, 10, 14, 41; his *History of Egypt*, 32 ff.; *Egypt and Syria from the Tell el-Amarna Letters*, 33 ff.; discovers Egyptian inscription containing mention of Israel, 38-9; demonstrates the archaeological importance of pottery, 81.
Philistine graves, probable, found at Gezer, 73.
Philology, rise of, 12-13.
'Pillars', or standing-stones, of the Old Testament, 62, 64.
Pinches, T. G., 18 n., 24, 25-6.
Pithom, discovery of site of, 26.
Pottery, archaeological value of, 42, 44-5, 81, 83, 84, 86.

Rameses II, 37.
Ramsay, Sir W. M., 8.
Rawlinson, Sir H. C., decipherer of cuneiform inscriptions, 4-6, 17-20, 22, 24, 25 n.
Religion of Israel, relation of, to those of neighbouring peoples, 16, 90.
Rhodian wine-jars found at Sandaḥannah and Gezer, 77-8; at Jericho, 92.
Robinson, Edward, traveller in Palestine, 8-9.
Rogers, Prof. R. W., *History of Babylonia and Assyria*, 4 n.; *Religion of Assyria and Babylonia, especially in its relation to Israel*, 90 n.

INDEX 95

Sachau, Prof., 29.
Samaria, excavation of site of, begun, 11.
Sandaḥannah, Tell, 10, 41, 65 n., 74, 77.
Sanskrit, discovery of, 13.
Sargon, 18.
Sayce, Prof., *Archaeology of the Cuneiform Inscriptions*, 35 n.; on stamped jar-handles, 76.
Schumacher, Dr. G., excavations at Tell el-Mutesellim (Megiddo), 10, with n., 67.
Sellin, Prof., excavations at Tell Ta'annek, 80–6; works describing them, 10 n.; finds Astarte-figures there, 57, 83, 84; *brochure* on the results of excavation in the East for our knowledge of the development of the religion of Israel, 86 n.; excavates Jericho, 91–2.
Sennacherib, 19–20, 45.
Septuagint, Greek of the, 15.
Seti I, expedition through Canaan, 37.
Simon Maccabaeus, castle of, at Gezer, 79–80.
Sinaitic Peninsula, survey of, 9.
Smith, George, 18, 20 n, 22–3.
Smith, Prof. George Adam, 9–10, 31, 37, 47.
Socoh, 74, 92.
'Standing-stones', 62; at Gezer, 64, 65; at Taanach, 65, 84; at Tell el-Mutesellim, 65.
Stanley, Dean, 9, 31.
Stones, believed to have been the abode of a deity, 65.

Taanach, excavation of, 10, 80–6.
Taanach and Megiddo, notices of, in the Old Testament, 80–1.
Tartan, meaning of the term discovered by Hincks, 20.

Tell, meaning of word, 41.
Tell ej-Judeideh, 10, 41, 74.
Tell el-Amarna, 15; the letters found there, 15, 32 ff., 44.
Tell el-Ḥesy (Lachish), 10, 40; excavation of, 41–5; cuneiform inscription found at, 42, 44.
Tell el-Mutesellim (Megiddo), 10.
Tell es-Ṣâfi, 10, 40, 65 n., 74.
Tell Sandaḥannah, 10, 41, 65 n., 74, 77.
Tell Zahariya, 10, 41, 74.
Thothmes III, 33; mentions Gezer, 47; Taanach and Megiddo, 80.
Travels of a Mohar, The, 38.
Troglodyte inhabitants of Gezer, 51, 52.
Tunnel, remarkable subterranean one found in Gezer, 52–3.

Versions, Ancient, value of, for recovering the original text of the Old Testament, 11.
Vincent, Père, his *Canaan d'après l'exploration récente*, 51 n.

Walls of Gezer, the, 54–6; of Jericho, 92.
Warren, Capt., 9.
Wilkinson, Gardner, *Manners and Customs of the Ancient Egyptians*, 4 n.
Winckler, Prof. Hugo, 34 n., 35 n.; excavations at Boghaz-keui by, 31, 38.

Young, Dr. Thomas, services to Egyptology, 3.

Zar'a (Ẓor'ah), high place at, 65.
Zimmern, Prof. H., 37.
Zimrida, governor of Lachish, 44.
Ziph, 74.

www.ingramcontent.com/pod-product-compliance
Lightning Source LLC
Chambersburg PA
CBHW050825160426
43192CB00010B/1901